Through Angela's Eye

Through Angela's Eye

The inside story of Operation Firewall

The largest identity theft case in United States history!

Always keep a watchful eye

Angela

Angela Hart

To order additional copies of this book, contact:
Xlibris Corporation
1-888-795-4274
www.Xlibris.com
Orders@Xlibris.com
81071

Contents

DEDICATION

This book is dedicated to the many victims of identity theft that was committed through their personal computer in the privacy of their own home! The purpose of writing this book is to help inform the average person who owns a personal computer how to protect oneself from identity theft. By exposing some of the dangers and risks involved with owning such an item, perhaps people could avoid going through a similar experience.

The experiences documented in this book are meant to help instruct people about the use of computers. By understanding how they operate, it will help people see what they are capable of. Hopefully, people will be better equipped to protect their financial data as well as their personal lives. Although many people have good intentions with the use of their computers, there are some out there, who have bad thoughts and intentions. In fact, a hacker can turn a person's computer into a weapon without them knowing. In some cases, it could look like the victim committed the crime when in fact they had no knowledge of the crime that was being committed.

Here are my hopes for the book.

- Children—learn to protect yourself from the dangers of the Internet.
- Parents—use this book as a tool to engage your children in healthful conversation about the dangers of the Internet, protect your privacy by monitoring your computer through different computer programs, take extra precautions by

disconnecting external connections to your computer, and learn the signs of identity theft that you need to look for.

- Financial institutions—take extra precautions when hiring those who work at your institution, and protect the consumer by going the extra distance, and do not expect the consumer to pay for additional expenses when it is your job to serve them.
- Corporations, companies and small businesses—take back control of your business away from the greedy hands of this government.
- Military personnel, families of prisoners of war, and families of those who died for their country—learn about what you can trust from the government you serve.
- Media—do better research when reporting a story, including presenting both sides of the story, especially if it comes through the Associated Press!

Although there may be men in powerful positions, this story is meant to give courage to those who may face similar insurmountable situations in their lives. It is also meant to expose the truth. Intuition, common sense, and plain old good investigating led to the arrests of most of those committing the crimes. However, two of the main people in this story have not been prosecuted yet as well as those who were involved the illegal purchase of the plates that are used to make every form of identification for the United States. It is my determination and will that something be done to these criminals! Sometimes, hiding behind the guise of the "witness protection program" does not protect those who are in pursuit of the truth and justice, but it protects those who are trying to hide their sinister secrets instead. Those who are in the "Domestic Spy Program" are unwilling participants and lack the protection of their rights.

Since I am under no contractual arrangements, which means that I was not in the "witness protection program" and never was with this government, I am free to tell my story. If I was truly being protected by them, they would have had to supply me with a written contract and told me what my rights were. Since they did not do this, I guess that means I was part of the "Domestic Spy Program", which was one of the over four thousand investigations that resulted from Operation Firewall. In a way, by the government not following their own rules and regulations, it has given me the freedom to tell my story.

What started out as a conspiracy theory has ended up as the God-honest truth! After reading this book, you will be able to draw your own conclusions. You cannot believe everything you hear or see on the news since the government controls the propaganda that is filtered through the guise of the Associated Press.

In addition, this book is dedicated to the many people including the investigators, law enforcement, agents, and undercover agents who were involved in the apprehension of these criminals. Thanks also go out to those within the government who were instrumental in creating new laws and passing them in order to charge them with the crimes.

There are many victims who were involved in this case. This book is dedicated to all people who were victims of these crimes. Even though this is a story about identity theft, I was legally advised to use a pen name on the book, which was against my wishes. However, it is more important to me to get the truth out. Although most of the other names and usernames as well as locations have been fictionalized in this book to protect those involved, the story is based on all written and preserved documentation of events. The chats used in this book remain unedited and may contain spelling mistakes which were left in order to keep them authentic. The usernames that are referred to in the story are **NOT** in use by any of the original people involved in this case. My accounts have all been stolen. Hopefully, this book will serve as a vindication for all of our names and expose how the crimes were committed and who perpetrated them.

Now here is the inside story of Operation Firewall as told *Through Angela's Eye.*

Chapter 1

The "Design-a-Site" Escapade

*B*eginning a new life after a nasty divorce and serious back injury, I was on the road to recovery. Investing in a new Web site looked like a viable way to have an income and work from the comforts of my own home. After years of being in my own business, I decided to hike down the same trail, this time opening an online Internet store. Always having a love for dancing, I decided to purchase a Web builder online. My goal was to make Footloose and Fancy Feet, the new Web site name, the largest one-stop shop for all your dancing needs. Everything from dance footwear, to training equipment, to jewelry, to makeup, and to costumes could all be purchased at my site. Future additions to my site included a blog and the largest dancing clip art collection.

Then I received a surprising phone call . . . a telemarketer calling me about a Web builder. The timing of the phone call could not have been any better, or so I thought. To this day, I still do not know how they got my name and number to contact me. Nor do I know how they knew I was in the market for a Web builder. I can only assume that they already hacked into my computer and saw the Web sites that I visited or they hacked into the Web site I had visited. After numerous conversations and negotiating, I finally made the purchase. Now I had a Web site to build.

Starting an online business was taking a long time. Little did I realize that the company I had purchased the Web site builder from had also stolen my identity! I went online to research the company and found that many complaints had been filed against them. I decided to keep a diary of the events in my identity theft case. It was not until I read numerous complaints on the Internet about this company, that I realized I too was a victim of theirs.

My story was similar to everyone else's that I was reading on the Internet. After initially responding to an e-mail about a book from well renowned businessman, I received a phone call from "Design-a-Site" about what they had to offer me. After being laid up for six years with a bad back, I was anxiously looking to start a business from my home. An internet store seemed to be a viable solution.

After a long discussion with Kato, a relentless salesman, he tried to sign me up for an expensive program, $13000. I refused. Then he came back with a cheaper program. He explained that I would still receive some of the $13000 program benefits. He explained that the website would be mine to do with as I pleased. Therefore, I signed up for the $10000 program on my credit card.

They said they sent me their catalog and starter materials, which I never received. However, my credit card was charged immediately which meant my payment was due immediately but I was using "Other People's Money" (OPM). This was their term they used to try to talk me into the purchase in the first place.

I already had an idea for a website selling dance clothing, costumes, accessories, footwear, jewelry, training equipment etc. So I would not be using their suppliers which meant that they would not get a kick back on any sales.

My package was to include the web-builder, accounting software, e-zine marketing campaign, banner ads, pop-up ads, business coaching, search engine optimization, guaranteed hits, and their warranty of service. My contract reads, "The condition of our warranty is based on you keeping your commitments. If after six months from today you have not recouped your initial investment of $10,035.00, we will continue to work with you an additional six months until you have done so."

Then they gave me the link for the web builder. What they neglected to tell me was that I had to do all the designing and building of the site. I had to get all the contacts for suppliers and negotiate with them. Then I had a phone consultation with my web design coach every week, which I did consistently. Within 15 weeks, I had built my site. My coach was teaching me from their online tutorial.

What I was not told initially was that all of the help they were providing for a substantial fee for their coaching was all available free links to websites that provided the tools I needed. They did not provide any of the help themselves. In fact, I have copies of their online tutorials. If you can read, then you don't need their coaches.

Initially I was charged a hosting fee of $31.95 a month from the inception of the purchase not when the site was actually up and running. I later found out that I could not move the site to another server since their shopping cart only worked on theirs, therefore guaranteeing them $31.95 per month.

Then I decided to go with my local bank for my merchant. However, I had incredible problems with trying to connect it since they were pushing their own merchant company so they get their kick back. After being persistent with them and contact with the proper agency, I got the merchant of my choice, my local bank.

Then it came time to use a different company to optimize my site. After six months of e-mails and phone calls, they did not live up to their marketing agreement. After spending hours on the phone with Kurt, he offered to switch me to a different company. I turned his offer down and asked for a refund. After Kurt hung up on the phone with me refusing to talk to me anymore, I contacted Kevin, an owner of the company supposedly. He offered to give me a refund toward the marketing on the program. So I was refunded half of my initial investment. By now almost a year had past, and I still did not recoup my initial investment. I did not even have an operational website.

In the meantime, several months earlier, I had contacted my new marketing people who came recommended by an associate of mine. They marketed and optimized my site to the best of their ability. However, "Design-a-Site" had lied to me telling me that this was a real website with HTML pages, when in fact only a few home pages were static; and the rest were dynamic or created on the fly. Therefore, it would be harder for search engines to pick up the pages since none of them were static.

Then in March of 2004, there was a plan to upgrade the shopping cart. When they did, my site went down for weeks, then months. After numerous phone calls to them of which they never answered, I then called them non-stop every extension until I reached a live person. They assured me that everything was up and running. However, their website pages did not reflect that either,

All I knew was that no one could place any orders from my site for those 3 months. The shopping cart that I had purchased could not be supported on their new server. Also, once they said it was completed, they took the accounting and tracking software away from me. That was in my contract and was the one deciding factor that helped me to decide on purchasing their product.

Customers e-mailed me saying they could not place orders, size and quantity selection boxes were messed up, orders were processed and lost but charged to their cards, and the list goes on! In addition, I needed to reconstruct all of the items that I was selling to a new web site. Since I had thousands of items to reenter, it would take me weeks if not months to complete.

After many more phone calls, they sent me an e-mail to sign, which I refused! However, they sent me another partial refund check. I was not done with them yet. It only made me want to keep looking for people to join me in a class action suit against them. I am not going to accept a partial settlement.

I wanted a full refund, as well as the promised doubling of my initial investment, as well as the cost of hiring someone new to reconstruct and move my website since their shopping cart was not compatible with any other server, and the lost sales for the down time, and something for the aggravation they put me through! They cannot change their minds as they go along. We had a contract, which they did not live up to! I could not let this issue go.

In fact, you might be interested in knowing that they probably purchased credit card information from members now arrested for trafficking over 1.7 million stolen credit card numbers. The hackers were targeting e-commerce sites. When I was first called, they already knew how much I had available on my credit and how much was in my bank account. My identity was stolen sometime prior to April of 2003.

No one can make you sign your rights away to sue them like they had tried to have me sign. In fact, there was nothing in my contract about any cancellation fee. They made up the rules as they went along. Percentages for cancellation varied amongst the people. Costs of the program varied based on how much credit you have available, how easily deceived you may be (if you aren't, they lower the price until you bite), and I can go on if you would like.

My next stop is the FTC and Attorney General. I think with all of my documentation, they will have a field day with this scam. Remember, my identity was stolen because my computer was hacked. The FBI and Secret Service have caught the hackers and have taken their computers. Eventually, the road will lead to justice. I suggested that they turn themselves in if they had any illegal dealings in securing names and financial information of their targeted victims.

It does not matter that someone may have signed a piece of "illegal" paper with them not to pursue them. I never signed one. Even if someone did, no one can force you to sign your rights away. In fact, they may even be entitled to a full refund. These events have put me in the pursuit of justice.

A short time later, I received the following response to the concerns that I presented to them.

> "As general counsel for the company in issue, I am surprised to see this complaint. A review of Ms. Hart's case with the company shows that she received assistance 32 times. Notwithstanding all of the services provided, Ms. Hart received a refund of her purchase price less the standard 20% restocking fee. As with any large company, there are times when there will be dissatisfied customers. We take prompt action to resolve customer issues, as was done in this case. There are a number of libelous statements made in this letter and we will be reviewing the same for appropriate legal action."

Then I made the following post in response. Since my letter to them, they have changed their old technical website every day. They deleted the bug list page but there are several copies floating around. Then they moved their home page to the news page and replaced the home page with the customer care page. Unknowingly, they posted a username and password on this page. I believe it was someone's login information. The text was login: skillmaster8421 password: gotcha42. I would like to clarify that and say "GOTCHA" to them. Guess what? That page has been totally deleted from their website! Once again, there are copies of that website page floating around. I also have eyewitnesses (thanks guys!) that saw these pages and have copies of these pages changing every day.

You would also be interested to know that once again changed their name. It is now the Treasury. If they have nothing to hide, why have they changed their name 3 times in the past year? Why did they change their old tech website, every day since I sent them my letter when they were "phasing out of that website" and try to delete incriminating evidence?

I would like to thank them for putting everything down in writing. It has made it easier for me to pursue legal action against them. If they thought that threatening me would scare me off since my identity was stolen last year, they are wrong! In fact, I would like to say that my identity is being heavily watched right now. Bad move! In fact, I think that they are now liable for trying to bring harm to me by threatening me. I have informed my attorney of these new developments.

In addition, I would suggest that they carefully reread my letter and pay attention to the wording that was used. I never accused them of anything. All I listed in the posting was the facts. I have documented proof to back up everything I experienced through that company. In fact, they should read our contract. There is no "restocking fee." In fact, their e-mail to me said "cancellation fee." Well, guess what? There is no mention of a cancellation fee in my contract either. In fact, they told me there was no cancellation. They promised to work with me until I made all of my money back and doubled it. Also, I phoned them more than 32 times! With all of the problems I was having, they kept passing me to everyone.

A genuine legal counsel or legal representative would not have threatened me by posting my identity. This shows intent to harm. By the way, according to them, they do not know this so-called "Reese's" last name. She only works on occasion. She only works on Tuesdays and Fridays now supposedly. She has no extension to leave a message. You can leave one with one of their salespeople to reach her. After researching the numerous posts on the Internet, I noticed that last names and first names were slightly different.

I tried to find out who owned this company. It is very hard to find but I finally did. There were several names and different addresses all over the place. They have changed their name so many times, that it is hard to keep track of. The reason they answer their phone "Corporate Headquarters" may be their way of trying to keep up with all of their many business names. There are too many names that were linked together through these numerous websites. Many of them had reports filed against them.

For a supposedly big business, which they painted themselves to be, I began to wonder if they are competent at all. When I first signed up, they only had two thousand websites they were hosting. The majority of their websites were adult oriented. Most of those sites that were up originally when I started my website were now down since they upgraded their server and people received partial refunds. Also, when I went to Google and typed in keywords like the company's name and state, complaints, fraud, scams, and any of the "other" names in different combinations and any other states of your choice, you would not believe all of the complaints filed against this company.

As far as the "services" provided, the only services I received from them was a big headache and a huge hole in my pocket! The coaching sessions were done from their online tutorials. If you did your homework and read them, you did not need a coach. I have a fully printed copy of their online tutorial to all the free links available on the internet. The accounting and tracking software was taken away from me. The marketing never happened. The website was down for months. I spent a lot of time spinning my wheels with a worthless website until I had it redone and moved to another server. So what "services" did they give me besides fleecing me? As far as giving me a full refund, to the contrary I have yet to receive the balance of my refund.

In fact, when I went to their website, the one that they were "phasing out of," I noticed that they had no choice but to abandon their old site since it was not supported by their new server. The same is true of their shopping cart website.

Changing their business name will not hide what they are doing! I will make sure I get all of my money back. My goal is to inform the public about this group of what I believe to be incompetent webhosts looking to phish for innocent people looking to make money by making a smart business investment. Let the people do their own research on the internet and decide for themselves. If I can spare anyone else from going through what I went through, then going through this was worth it.

I was blatantly lied to by "Design-a-Site". They did not provide the services I was promised. My web site could not be found and was down or not working properly from the day it was put up until the day I cancelled with them. Ultimately, I lost both time and money. I could have chalked a lot of it up to an education if it were not for all of the nonsense this company put me through.

Then came a startling response by someone who knew the right legal terms to put "Design-a-Site" back in their place.

> "If your legal department would consider that you read the requisites and that what was stated along with the facts were opinionated criticism and not libelous. If she was the "rare" dissatisfied customer, that had been properly refunded, then you would have nothing to worry about.
>
> I came across some interesting information. I do find it interesting that you jumped on this so quickly. It was probably a good move. While researching an old problem with someone else's internet business-gone bad, you will see how things can snowball with real scams and deceptive practices. There were some similarities that might tie you to those entities due to crossed web searches. Oddly enough the Internet business that had gone bad had an individual that was believed to be associated with the mentoring group "Teachers In Business, Inc. (TIB)." That person also had IT background like some who worked for them had. The "re-sellers" sold an internet business that had problems on many levels which caused the web based business to not be realistically operable as a business."

I had decided to place my story online in the hopes of helping other people. Numerous postings went up in support. One woman was so grateful that she had come across my posting, that she was able to quickly send an email of cancellation to them and before that talked to her credit card company and told them what happened. She too had been told that her conversation had been recorded when she was agreeing to the 'contract'.

> Well it looks like they have a problem. If those they represent are not taking care of things at base level then they will see more of these complaints. When you take people's money and push them too far, any legal

threats have no meaning to them. They also run the risk of waking up people that may be unaware of similar problems that they may have that parallel mine. What has all the elements of a scam but is not a scam?

Then Kevin wanted to address the following to me.
It seems most of the people that posted here are not out to report facts, but rather their stories that are blined by anger and frustratation at perhaps a company or a person or themselves that are driving them attack blindly and if the truth is a casualty
Angela,
I want to cover some of the points in the information that you posted.

Angela—I contacted Kevin, an owner of the company supposedly. He offered to give me a refund toward the marketing on the program. So I was refunded half of my initial investment.

*I have always been clear what my role in this company has been for the last three years, I have been the Customer Care (now Student care) Manager.

*We refunded you all of your money minus 20% for coaching services. You received Five extra coaching session to help you make up two session you failed to show up for with your coach.
(If you sign a disclosure document, I can post all the coaching notes with dates and times)

Angela—go to Google and type in keywords like "Design-a-Site", complaints, fraud, Utah, Texas, Florida, scams, and any of the aforementioned names in different combinations and any other states of your choice.

*O.K This is a fair request: Google search

http://www.google.com/search?hl=en&q=Design-a-Site&btnG=Google+Search (Nothing negative)
Please read the full report. There is nothing negative about "Design-a-Site"

*When asked if they felt the stories on the website were true they pointed to the Disclaimer on their website:

"The personal experiences listed on this page are the experiences of users unfamiliar to us. We have no way to verify the validity of these claims and you the decision maker should take the hearsay nature of these statements into account when reading them . . ."

*To use this link as a way to prove our company is somehow treating people wrongly is intellectually dishonest of you. We will not even validate the stories as truth.

* I think this is a great resource it has pros and cons of the program. I encourage all to read all the posts.

It seems you always focus on the negative. Is your glass half empty or half full? Mine's half full and I'm working to fill it further.

Complainers like you are usually good at stating problems in such an accusing manner that it is hard to sort out the true problems from the complaints. Complainers tend to blame others when something goes wrong. They feel powerless to fix the things they complain about. They rely on others to fix things because this allows them to believe that they are free of faults. This seems to be the way you are coming off on the place . . ."

*This redirects you to http://www.Design-a-Site.com.

Angela—A genuine legal counsel or legal representative would not have posted my last name. Posting my last name shows intent to harm. By the way, according to "Design-a-Site" they do not know this so-called "Reese's" last name. She only works on occasion. She only works on Tuesdays and Fridays now supposedly. She has no extension to leave a message. You can leave one with Jeff to reach her.

* Angela,—Reese is "Design-a-Site's" Legal Counsel. To contact her all you needed to do is contact me and I could have helped you. I know you have my contact information, but in case you do not have it here it is.

Then he listed his contact information.

It is our goal to help people and I am sorry to see that it did not work for Angela.

I do have the opportunity to talk with our students every day and see the success stories. We really care about our students and care about their success.

It hurts me personally to read the things that have been written here. Especially when I know many of them to be false, and that is why I am taking time to respond. I and everyone I work with take seriously the following commitments.

I am a success story myself. I guess that is why this is why I feel bad that it did not work out for Angela. I am using the same site and system and am very happy.

I want to end this post with a promise to all. We will do what is fair and honest. I truly feel we did what was fair and honest in this case with Angela. And I wish her the best in life.

Please feel free to contact me at home or work I plan on being here with this company for a very long time."

Now he really pushed by buttons. I have documentation to back up all the facts listed.

Fact 1:
A program was sold to me be based on my "available credit limit"

Fact 2:
I never received my initial packet of goods and a tape recording of my "verbal contract." I do not know if anyone has received that.

Fact 3:
The online tutorial and coaching was a list of all the free links on the internet.

Fact 4:
They provided me with a website that only worked on their server.

Fact 5:
I had trouble setting up my merchant account with my local bank. They will verify that.

Fact 6:
They lied to me by telling me that the website was HTML when in fact it was dynamic. My webmaster was privy to that conversation.

Fact 7:
They never optimized or marketed my website even after months of trying to contact them by phone and e-mail.

Fact 8:

According to the Edgar postings, the advice they received for the upgrade of the server failed. The dates of the postings were prior to the upgrade of the server. In fact, my shopping cart and website could not be supported on the new server. Records of other users or client's websites and the web pages that they removed substantiate this. My site was down for 3 months. In fact, I moved my domain and had to have the website rebuilt. Even after I did this, my account was continuing to be billed the $31.95 hosting fee for 4 months even though I no longer had my site with them. I eventually had to close my bank account to stop the charges. My bank statements verify this.

They started changing their old website by removing the "bug list," which listed all the problems people were having with their websites that were on the previous server and would not function on their new server as well as other pages. Their phones rang off the hook, which no one ever answered during this time-period. People sent hundreds or thousands of e-mails trying to find out what was going on. Then "Design-a-Site" had the problem that new clients would not sign up when they saw the list of bugs with their site. Next, they had to create a new site for the new server for their new clients thus "phasing out" of the existing website. Copies of the previous web pages that they removed from their old site have been copied and saved for future reference.

Fact 10:
They have changed their name once again.

Fact 11:
"Design-a-Site" posted my name! If they thought that posting my last name would scare me off since my identity was stolen last year, they are dead wrong! In fact, I would like to say that my identity is being

"heavily" watched right now. Bad move! In fact, I think that they are now liable for trying to bring harm to me by posting my last name. If you do not believe me, read the above.

Fact 12:
My contract has no mention of a "restocking fee" or "cancellation fee" or now a "coaching fee." I have the contract.

Fact 13:
Reese identified herself as "general counsel" not "legal counsel" as Kevin says. She will not even come forward to talk to me by identifying her full name and contact information, but she was terribly quick to post my identity out there. Now Kevin is responding to me. What happened to Reese? Does she even exist?

Fact 14:
I found that Design-a-Site's program was very limiting. Everything that is included in their product or package is owned by them. Then you run into the problem of trying to move it elsewhere. There seems to be much better deals out there. Most of what you are supplied with can be found on the internet for no charge. In addition, hosting costs are usually cheaper anywhere else, like $5-$10 per month. There are shopping carts out there that will work on just about any server. If you have a problem with your site and need to move it to another server, in a matter of a few minutes your site is back up and open for business. You can also purchase upgrades for the website to customize it for you. This includes gift certificate option, promotional code option, accounting/tax option and others.

Fact 15:
Then I ran into the problem that their server was not secure. Anyone could view everyone's personal credit

card information from the back end of their system; that is anyone who works for them. In addition, when my computer was hacked, the hackers could view everyone's information right from my own computer screen since I could view it all. It was a good thing I discovered the hack before the store went live! On a secure site, you can only see the last 4 digits of the card, no expiration date, a transaction number, the date and the amount. At that point, even if your computer was hacked, no one would be able to see anyone's credit card information. That secures the purchasers personal and financial information. Only the merchant themselves can see all of the information; full account information, number, and expiration date. Two ways to know that a site is secure is to look for the little "lock" icon and the web address starts with https, s=secure.

The reason I went with my local bank as my merchant is that I wanted to know who was handling my money. After I thought about it, I did not like them seeing my accounting software for the business on their server. It is not a good practice to post your financial information anywhere on the internet or on a server. The program I have now transfers order information right into Quickbooks or Peachtree and for a fraction of the price. Therefore, my host does not see any of my expenses or actual checkbook as they did on their server. Therefore, they cannot see the bottom line or anything going on in any other bank accounts.

Fact 16:
My initial "bait" came from the purchase of an e-book. It was after this purchase that I was contacted by them. I would like to know how they got my e-mail address since I did not sign up for anything until after I received their e-mail. The "switch" came when they phoned me. My credit card receipt and initial e-mail prove this.

Reese: "As general counsel for the company in issue, I am surprised to see this posting. A review of Ms. Hart's case with the company shows that she received assistance 32 times. Notwithstanding all of the services provided, Ms. Hart received a refund of her purchase price less the standard 20% restocking fee. As with any large company, there are times when there will be dissatisfied customers. We take prompt action to resolve customer issues, as was done in this case. There are a number of libelous statements made in this posting and we will be reviewing the same for appropriate legal action."

I really wish they would get their story straight. Reese said that I "received a refund of her purchase price less the standard 20% restocking fee." Now Kevin is saying, "We refunded you all of your money minus 20% for "coaching services." You received five extra coaching sessions to help you make up two sessions you failed to show up for with your coach." Just for the record, I never missed a coaching session. There was only one session that I had to reschedule and one that my coach rescheduled due to scheduling conflicts, which occurred a few days in advance of the scheduled time. I did not receive an extra five coaching sessions! Besides, why would you give me 5 more sessions if I missed 2? Also, I wish they would get your story straight. Was it a 20% restocking fee or 20% coaching services or 20% cancellation fee as per my e-mail? Some people received a full refund, some less a 10% cancellation fee, some 15%, 20% and so on. Others received a full refund less a "restocking fee" or "coaching fee." None of these fees are even mentioned in my written contract. Therefore, I have not received a full refund. In fact, since I had to have my site rebuilt and moved, they are responsible for all of my time that I put into their useless site, for the construction of the new site, as well as all of the hosting fees, interest payments on my credit card, and any out-of-pocket expenses related to this venture. Therefore, I am still awaiting a full refund. Something for all the aggravation would be nice too. I will not hold my breath.

They told me the following. "It seems most of the people that posted here are not out to report facts, but rather their stories that are *blined* by anger and *frustratation* at perhaps a company or a person or themselves that are driving them attack blindly and if the truth is a casualty" (Notice that blinded and frustration are spelled wrong. I wonder who is blinded and frustrated.)

They did get one thing right. I am angry. I am angry that they had taken advantage of many people. I did not like being "blown-off" especially after I spent so much money on this program. The only people they care about are themselves and their pocketbook! Since this posting as well as numerous others, they are losing some business. Now they are going to respond to me in a "nice" way after they attacked me and threatened me? They should have thought about what they were going to say before they threatened me. Bad move! If they had listened to me in the beginning, I would not have had to push the matter this far.

I find it odd that no one has posted anything on the internet about being "turned down" by them. Perhaps, that is because they know your credit and bank history before they contact you. They do not waste any time calling people who do not have the money. I know in my case, they knew how much "available credit" I had since their first offer of $13000 happened to be all that I had available on that card.

Also, Kevin, if your website is so successful, why are you still working for "Design-a-Site"? I think you should get the website off the ground quick just in case they go out of business. As a side note, if "Design-a-Site" in a google search does not bring back anything negative try "Design-a-Site" mentors or any other combination of names and try reading the first 10 pages and try other terms as I suggested in a previous post. You might be surprised how many negative reports are out there about all your "entities."

I think the people working for them better go back to school. Their grammar and language is not befitting for a "big" company. In addition, Reese needs to go back to law school and finish getting her degree before she threatens people. They forget that most of the people they talked into purchasing their products they sold on the fact that this was an "investment" and there was a lot of work involved and that it was "not a get rich quick scheme." That means that they are dealing with people who can think for themselves not those who work for other businesses and cannot think for themselves.

By the way, how can we verify any of your "success stories"? How can we know that you did not write them or that the people even exist? Even if you could call the people, how do we know if they are legit and that they do not work for you? After all the lies this company told me, I would not trust anything they say.

For the record, I am not a complainer who blames others when something goes wrong. If it is my fault, I accept responsibility. "Design-a-Site" had the server that would not work after the upgrade. "Design-a-Site" never optimized my site. "Design-a-Site" took the accounting software away from me. "Design-a-Site" overcharged my bank account for hosting fees after the site moved to another server. "Design-a-Site" lied to me about the site being HTML not dynamic. In fact,

I had the website rebuilt and moved so that it does work. I have had a few minor problems with the site. I certainly do not know everything about building a site. That is why I hired a new webmaster. I pay for this service and they deliver, unlike this company. I think "Design-a-Site" should own up to their faults and stop blaming everyone else.

In addition, Reid had problems with a similar program through a different company, a division of this company. Even though "Design-a-Site" did not deal with him directly, they support and push the Mentoring program and make money off it. That makes "Design-a-Site" responsible for his problems, not me!

Then I told them, "I find it funny that you are now asking me to sign a disclosure. Why are you asking now? You exposed my name without my permission. For the record, I AM NOT SIGNING ANYTHING! If I were you, I would watch my step closely and BACK OFF!"

There seems to be a lot of "identity theft" going on here. "Design-a-Site" had my personal and financial information before they ever contacted me. They are hiding their identity by hiding behind so many business names as well as different phone numbers and addresses. They also had access to thousands of names and personal and financial information from anyone who purchased anything from any of the websites they host. Their names differ slightly from other names people have posted. Reese does not have a last name. Does she even exist? Too bad they cannot produce her. Now I have to deal with Kevin. Is it Kevin Winston or Kevin Wilston or something altogether different? I think not. They can deal with my attorney. It is a little too late to talk, especially after they attacked me.

My advice to anyone who is having dealings with this company is close all your credit card accounts. Get a new number assigned for each card you have since you do not know how much credit information might be out there. Change any passwords too. Then get copies of your credit reports from the 3 major companies, Equifax, Trans Union, and Experian. By placing a "fraud alert" on your credit you can receive free copies of your credit report. Scan your computers for Trojans and Keyloggers. Put on an anti-virus program and firewall. Buy a router, which is a hardware firewall and will not allow anything to pass through it without your permission. This is the best and cheapest investment to secure your computer and I highly recommend it. Purchase a router for $30-$75 at Radio Shack or any other electronic store. Download a free or paid spy-ware program. Delete cookies from your computer on a daily basis. Get a new e-mail account. Close the old one and assign a completely different password that is not a pet or child's name, birth date, phone number, social security number, or any other previously used password. A combination of letters and numbers works best. There are some easy fixes to do to your computer to ensure that no one can take your personal information and steal your identity from under your nose. Although you can order from a secure site, it does not ensure you that your computer is secure. By the way, recent hacking attempts on my computer have not worked, nor will they.

Reid, I think you missed the point I was trying to make by listing all of the above names. (The business names have been changed or omitted.) I did a search on this site for "Design-a-Site". ALL of these names listed on these reports linked to "Design-a-Site's name, including that mentoring program! That means that "Design-a-Site" is behind ALL of these scams in one way or another.

The purpose of me listing all of the names to this posting of "Design-a-Site" is to link this page to all of those other names that they promote. This way, people will be able to see that "Design-a-Site" is behind a multitude of the "business entities" here. Although each "business entity" may not be that big of a business, if you combine the fraudulent income of all of these businesses, I believe this is one of the biggest cons going around!

I believe that anyone who these "business entities" contacted has had their identity stolen. When someone's identity is stolen, most cases go unreported simply because the victim is not aware that someone has stolen their identity.

In this case, instead of "Design-a-Site" actually fraudulently charging your credit card, they are persuading you to give them the information to fleece you. In the end, they still end up with the money. They neglect to tell you that they already had your credit information before they called you! Unless you had someone new calling you, who was in "training," slip up and admit to the cost of the program being the same dollar amount of credit you had available (like in my case), you would not know your identity was stolen. I did think it was odd that the $13000 cost of the program happened to be the amount of "available credit" on my credit card but I could not make the connection that my identity had been hacked or stolen until I found out my computer was hacked. Most people do not know much about computer security. They do not know how easily someone can take their identity from right under their nose. I certainly did not know until it was too late. The computer hack was how they gained my e-mail address for the initial bait as well as all of my personal information.

Now all I can do is inform the public about my ordeal and maybe prevent it happening to others. In this case, it seems that I may be "waking up" people to the fact that they too might have been a victim of identity theft.

Then I researched the Federal statutes regarding bait advertising and deception. I came across the Code of Federal Regulations, Title 16, Part 238

"The primary aim of a bait advertisement is to obtain leads as to persons interested in buying merchandise of the type so advertised"

Code of Federal Regulations, Title 16, Part 238.2(b)

"Even though the true facts are subsequently made known to the viewer, the law is violated if the first contact or interview is secured by deception."

Since this company used "bait advertisements" and "deception" as defined by the Code of Federal Regulations and solicits and does business across state lines, they violate Federal fraud statutes.

Then a response to Design-a-Site's general counsel's posting came.

"This rebuttal is meant specifically as a response to Reese's comments made to Angela on 1/4/2005. I too feel that my partners and I have been scammed by "Design-a-Site". We have tried to receive a refund and I/we were quite surprised by some of the statements made in Reese's posting. Reese stated that when she reviewed Angela's file, it showed that Angela had received assistance from the company 32 times. For all intents and purposes, that doesn't mean a whole lot. When my partners and I felt scammed and requested a refund, we were told that our file stated numerous things that were very misleading. I don't trust what is stated in the "files." Our mentor, Randall, reported in our file that we failed to complete our weekly homework assignments. However, he never gave us any to complete.

In addition, Reese stated that Angela received a refund and that "Design-a-Site" takes "prompt action to resolve customer issues." When my partners and I tried to get our money refunded, we were told by Kevin Winston that "Design-a-Site" does not give refunds. This is obviously untrue. We tried speaking with Mr. Winston about our unhappiness with the program, but we were treated rudely and felt that our concerns were dismissed. If "Design-a-Site" is prompt in handling customer concerns, why haven't we received a refund? I have sent several emails to various people at "Design-a-Site" voicing my concerns and have not heard a response from one of them. I do not consider that prompt or anywhere remotely close to customer service."

Then Kevin, aka Arron, decided to put his two cents in. "After reading all the complaints contained here, one is expected to believe that all institutions and organizations for higher education and knowledge gathering which charge a fee are rip-offs. As with any education and investment, you reap what you *soe* that includes investigating what you are putting your time and money into. Also, never expect others to do all of the work for you and then believe that the rewards will just come flooding in.
With regard to the question of, why would someone agree to help others start up their own business? Why not just seize the opportunity and increase one's own profits rather than help someone else? Remember the phrase, "What goes around, comes around"? Or how about the charitable philosophy of what you give will come back to you ten-fold. (Now

that one can be for positive results and negative.) Most extremely successful people will tell you that the greatest success is that which is gained through helping others to succeed. Examples are the following families: Rockefeller, Ford, Carnegie, DuPont, Walton, Vanderbilt, and many more too numerous to mention here. As these families have contributed to charity and assisting others to succeed, their fortunes have increased exponentially.

I myself have never done business with any of the organizations that have been ripped on in this report, but I am even more inclined to do so given the tone of most of the *writtings* here. I am looking to start a new company which will assist others to find financial freedom. If an I-Works affiliate or subsidiary can help me to help those others reach their dreams, then I will gladly accept that help and the cost will be *negligable* compared to the benefit."

Then I sent them the following e-mail.

"Bad move "Design-a-Site"!!! I told you to BACK OFF!!! You better CALL OFF YOUR HITMEN!

FYI: All e-mails and phone calls are being traced. You made a crucial mistake. You should have taken my advice and backed off already!!!

We know who you are. We have the IP addresses as well as the names and addresses that belong to those e-mails. We also have the name and address of the person belonging to the cell phone. We actually have the name of the real person using the cloned phone too as well as their personal information. Proxy servers do not work with the people watching my identity. You cannot hide behind AOL either or Yahoo! for that matter. There is no place to hide.

Did I mention? Really, really bad move!!! Threats do not scare me. BTW . . . there are sooooooooooooo many people watching my identity right now; I would not try anything foolish like before! That would be a REALLY, REALLY, REALLY BAD MOVE!

I hope you are watching the news "Design-a-Site"! They are changing all of the laws before they come for you and all of your crones (all of the other "business entities"). Time is almost up!

By the way, recent hacking attempts have not worked, nor will they! Keep trying though. It gives me more evidence."

I do not respond personally to any of the e-mails or phone calls I receive. All information is being passed through to the proper authorities and channels due to the nature of the threats I am receiving.

"*Arron*" is right. "Design-a-Site" is now going to "reap what you *soe*". That is why you are seeing all of the negative postings against them and the other "business entities." Their time has almost come.

Nice try "Design-a-Site"! I would like to say that the response "Design-a-Site" posted as "*Arron*" was well thought out. However, I would like to suggest to "Design-a-Site", next time to pick a name that they can spell. *Arron* is spelled Aaron. Try using spell check too.

"Design-a-Site" has not taken my advice and backed off. They keep on trying to contact me and send me messages through e-mail and these postings.

Maybe I should have been more specific in my previous posting. I told "Design-a-Site" to call off their hit men, when I should have said HITMNN007!!! I guess they do

NOT believe me when I say that my identity is being "HEAVILY WATCHED" by the real 007's.

That last posting was directed to "Design-a-Site" and their "HITMEN" as a reply to the e-mail threats and phone calls I have received.

BACK OFF "Design-a-Site"! If you are wondering why the tone of these last few writings is the way it is, it is because I DO NOT TAKE KINDLY TO THREATS!!! By the way, I do not take any bait that is put out in front of me no matter how nice the e-mail may sound. I am not replying to any of the e-mails people are sending me since I am protecting myself due to the fact that, "Design-a-Site" posted my name and identity!

"Design-a-Site", I suggest that if you have anything to say to me, YOU DO SO ON THIS FORUM! DO NOT CALL OR E-MAIL ME or USE ANYONE ELSE'S IDENTITY! All IP addresses of e-mails are being traced, as well as phone calls. By the way, proxy servers do NOT work with the people watching my identity. Did I mention, using cloned phones or someone else's phone does NOT work with them? Did you ever hear of satellites? NOW BACK OFF!

"Arron" was right when he said, "what goes around comes around." "Design-a-Site" and all of their "business entities" are now starting to see that deceiving and fleecing the public eventually will catch up to them.

I would like to thank this website for giving us a public forum to post complaints on. This is how we can vent and let everyone know what is going on about these corrupt mentoring companies. By comparing reports, we can see that we are not alone. Sites like this one help expose the corruption and hopefully, help others not to fall into the same trap. That is why "Design-a-Site" is angry now. It is finally starting to hit them in their pockets! About time since "Design-a-Site" and their "business entities" hit all of us in the pocket already! Remember what "*Arron*" said, "you reap what you *soe*" and "What goes around, comes around."

"Design-a-Site" and their "business entities" are about to reap what they have sown.

First of all, there were major issues contrary to what Kevin says. Search for yourself and you will discover many, many sites where people have filed complaints against "Design-a-Site" and their "business entities."

Second, Kevin's comment that people did not follow through on their commitments is not true. It was "Design-a-Site", who never did what they were supposed to do. I certainly did. My problems were all the fault of "Design-a-Site". This included a website that was not operational, a server that was always down, excess fees that were taken out of my bank account for services that had been cancelled, their marketing people never marketing my site, a shopping cart and website that could not be supported on the new server, their server that was not secure, and many other "commitment issues" that "Design-a-Site" ignored.

BREECH OF CONTRACT on behalf of "Design-a-Site" has led me to pursue justice against them for myself as well as anyone else who wants justice. They promised, in writing, to double my initial investment within 6 months. I spent well over a year trying to get "Design-a-Site" to get my site operational but could not. Then I decided to move my site to another server, which meant redoing all of the work I had put into my website.

Therefore, I was out my original investment of $10,035, my hours upon hours of time putting in my hundreds of products, the loss of sales for the 6 months of down time since my site was not marketed and optimized, the loss of sales for more than 3 months when "Design-a-Site's server was upgraded and could no longer support my site, the time and reconstruction of my website in order to get my site up and operational, and the promise to double my investment within the first 6 months. That would mean that since my site was not up for almost a year and a half, I should have been able to double by investment 3 times over!

Then "Design-a-Site" had the nerve to charge me a "restocking fee" or "cancellation fee" or now a "coaching fee." I have the contract. There is no mention of any type of fee for leaving "Design-a-Site". In fact, "Design-a-Site" had the whole web package bundled so that they profited off every angle. This meant that "Design-a-Site" made money off the web builder, the optimization which was a joke with dynamic pages, not HTML, the hosting fees, the merchant account that they were pushing, and any other expenses related to this venture. There was no way to leave "Design-a-Site" without losing everything. How dare they think of keeping any of my hard-earned money!

NON-DISCLOSURE of all the fees related to this venture, as well as the cost of "Design-a-Site's program at the initial contact is another federal statute "Design-a-Site" has broken.

SPYWARE helped "Design-a-Site" to obtain leads and people's personal information. Think about how you were contacted. The initial e-mail was sent or you phoned them after seeing an infomercial. After your initial purchase or bait, which was usually a book, they had your credit card information as well as your name and address. If you used the computer, they followed your internet habits and spied on you through the computer. This leads to

IDENTITY THEFT, which is another crime "Design-a-Site" probably committed. Think about what "Design-a-Site" or any other "business entity" of theirs first offered you the program for. Most likely it was the same as the amount of "available credit" you had on your credit card or how much you had in your bank account.

The SWITCH came when you were phoned by "Design-a-Site" or any of their other "business entities." This means that "Design-a-Site" violated another federal statute that of the "BAIT AND SWITCH" scheme.

To clarify how small "Design-a-Site" really is, when I was with them they only had about 2,000 websites up and running most of which are no longer working since they upgraded their server. I have a copy of their previous clients. That would mean that the majority of people who purchased from "Design-a-Site" or any of their "business entities" received a partial refund or no refund at all. However, if you combine the total fraudulent income from all of their "business entities," it is one of the biggest cons out there!

My questions are:

Why should "Design-a-Site" keep any of the money people invested into their fraudulent schemes especially if they hide behind many layers of "business entities" so that a person cannot find complaints about them on file since they search under the wrong name since they change their name constantly?

Why has "Design-a-Site" not addressed all of my questions?

Why has "Design-a-Site" not provided any proof of the unsubstantiated statements of their success stories?

Why will "Design-a-Site" not come forward to answer these questions? What are they hiding?

Why will "Design-a-Site" not refute any of the statements made? Perhaps they know they are true and realize they are not going to have a leg to stand on when they have to answer to federal authorities in court about their deception and fraudulent schemes.

Why will "Design-a-Site" not come out from hiding behind all of these "business entities" and continue to use different identities other than their own?

Contrary to what Kevin says, there is a unified consumer movement occurring. Thanks to this web site, e-mails have been flooding in to me. (Thanks for posting my identity "Design-a-Site"! Since I cannot hide, I will not let you either. Did I mention, bad move!) This web site also has a long list of people's names and contact information that the authorities have access to view. I have a long list of unsatisfied customers who have left "Design-a-Site" since their websites were not operational on their previous server. I have an even longer list of people who are not satisfied with any of their other "business entities" which includes a long list of almost 100 business names that are being used in this "web-mob's circle of deceit" and 1000's of people who were not satisfied. It takes a while to gather all of the information for such a lawsuit. It will take some time to sort through all of the 1000's of complaints on file with all agencies of all states such as the Attorney General's offices, BBB's, credit card companies, etc. Also, in class action lawsuits, many times the victim is only contacted in the end once a settlement has been reached. I have had many come forward to say that they are willing to use their story and testify if necessary.

"Design-a-Site" is trying to hide themselves as well as their deception and fraud. Did I mention earlier, "Design-a-Site", it does not work with the people watching your identity right now? So tell me "Design-a-Site", how does it feel to have someone watching your identity? Tables have now turned. The heat has been turned up now. Is it getting a little too hot for you? How does it feel to have the shoe on the other foot?

Now maybe, since it is hitting "Design-a-Site" in the pocket, they will know how their victims feel. Hopefully soon, they will have a lot of time to think about what they have done when they are all behind bars! Time is ticking away! I am happy to say to "Design-a-Site" that I am not going away until "Design-a-Site" and their "business entities" get what is coming to them. It should not be much longer.

I noticed when I tried to find "Design-a-Site" in the files of the Utah Better Business Bureau I was unsuccessful. I have since learned that they use Dream Big, Inc. and are also doing business as other business names.

Then one of the most amazing things happened. Someone figured out Reese's real identity! Since she had so graciously posted my identity, this person decided to post hers.

"Since "Reese" so graciously revealed Angela's last name, here is some information obtained through a search on the Internet and her connection to the FAA. Please note, Reese Shepherd may or may not be the "Reese" who submitted a rebuttal in this matter. Again, this information was obtained from an Internet search and its validity is unknown. The sources where this information was gathered are included.

According to the Utah State Bar Membership Public Address Locator, there is only one attorney named Reese

(Reese Suzanne Shepherd) in Utah. The Public Address Locator provides the following information:

Reese S Shepherd worked in estate planning in Sandy, Utah. Included was the address, phone number, and e-mail address of where she worked. They put in her membership information, the school she went to, and date graduated. The law firm that she originally worked for was also listed. Her schooling included estate planning, Federal taxation, and commercial law. Ms. Shepherd is an attorney specializing in estate planning and estate administration as well as business planning and trust formation. She has extensive experience in IRS related resolutions, trust formation, gift tax planning, family business formation, and general business planning.

She later worked as an executive in an Internet based company. Her new company was also listed which contained the contact information as well.

Finally some startling information came forward. Evidently, during the legal proceedings, some personal information became public knowledge. It appeared that Ms. Shepherd (Steuben) and Mr. Daniel R. Shepherd were divorced on May 17, 1990, after approximately one year and four months of marriage. Ms. Shepherd (Steuben) married Joseph Steuben in October, 1989. That's right. According to the Court's opinion, Ms. Shepherd (Steuben) married Mr. Shepherd January 16, 1987 in Springville, UT, married Mr. Steuben in October, 1989, and divorced Mr. Shepherd on May 17, 1990. Although this seems to be incorrect, those are the dates given by the Utah Court of Appeals. The Court stated, "Steuben married Joseph Steuben in October 1989 and later moved the court to enter a nunc pro tunc order that effectively granted the divorce between Steuben and Shepherd on June 26, 1989.

In July 1991, while living in Colorado, Steuben filed a petition for a change of surname on behalf of the minor child in an attempt to legally change the child's surname to Steuben. The trial court ruled in favor of Shepherd and ordered that the child retain the surname of Shepherd and that Steuben notify the child's school and church officials of the child's correct surname. Steuben appeal(ed) from the trial court's findings of fact, conclusions of law, and order.

The Utah Court of Appeals affirmed the trial court's ultimate conclusion that the child should continue to bear the surname Shepherd.

An endnote to the opinion states, "Steuben's interference with Shepherd's visitation rights has necessitated court intervention which ordered Steuben to allow Shepherd to see the child. Steuben was previously held in contempt for denying Shepherd visitation."

Before beginning a private practice of her own, Ms. Shepherd practiced with a law firm. She has also worked for the Utah Attorney General's Office, the Federal Aviation Administration in Longmont, Colorado and a Community School of Learning in Boulder, Colorado. She received her Juris Doctor Cum Laude from Brigham Young University and a Bachelor's of Science in Accounting from the University of the State of New York. For two years, Ms. Shepherd devoted time to the Tuesday Night Bar, a program providing free consultation, advice and referral to members of the community who otherwise did not have the means to pay for the services.

Ms. Shepherd's past employment with the Federal Aviation Administration is fascinating in light of the recent posts by Angela.

Joseph W Steuben and Joseph W. FAA both have ties to Raccoon Hollow Dr., Sandy, UT 84093. Could FAA be a typo for the Federal Aviation Administration?

There is a picture of Reese Shepherd, a 37-year old attorney who lives in Salt Lake City, on the website. It appears on one of the inside pages.

Again, Reese Shepherd may or may not be the "Reese" who submitted a rebuttal in this matter. This information was obtained from an Internet search and its validity is unknown.

Then an astute consumer wanted to clarify a few things that "Design-a-Site" was now doing to keep from being a bait, fish, hook, campaign. She said,

"They now ask you to call so you can get your "free gift". I too got taken by them. I do not know about all the stuff said to be fraudulent to get you to buy. Though if what other people have been saying about the laws is true (I'm sure it is) then they are definitely Frauds. (I bought a couple other things on line pertaining to grants, and writing grants, and got a call from a company helping with Grant Writing. It sounded just like "Design-a-Site" and is even in Utah. Someone might want to check that out.) But I do know that what you get for your money is not worth it. I would never have paid five hundred dollars for what I got.

Upon reading my "Agreement" with "Design-a-Site" I found that it tells you "You have the right to cancel for any reason within three days of your initial sign up to receive a full refund. Notification of cancellation must be received via email. Cancellation requests should be sent to activate@Design-a-Site-Mentors.com and must include your name, email address, and the reason for cancellation. You may cancel your account at any time after the first three days. All set-up and design charges will not be refunded for work already performed."

So I say that I want a refund and Kevin Winston calls me. We have a nice conversation where he offers me to start my mentoring phone calls over and with a new coach and if that doesn't work then we'll "negotiate a fair price for the mentoring already given". I say I have to talk to my husband about that he tells me go ahead. So then we play phone tag for 3 days. Kevin then goes on vacation; no e-mail or phone call telling me who he gave my case to.

But we had a very nice conversation and things sounded good.

Then I received a call yesterday and a guy from student care tells me he's calling to set up things with a new mentor.

I tell him we'd just like a refund and that Kevin said we'd negotiate one. He tells me "it is funny Kevin mentioned a refund since we don't give refunds." He told me he'd have to research the case more and talk to the board of directors and get back to me.

What a crock. It doesn't say you can't get a refund and I'll guarantee that the "set-up and design charges" were nowhere near what I paid the company.

It's been over 90 days and I don't think I can get my credit company to contest this. What can I do? If someone can tell me the case number of the suit that's going on by Angela, that would be so awesome. I'd then be able to keep an eye on how that is going.

As far as the promises go they don't deliver on any of that but I'd really just settle for getting the money off my credit card so that I can actually get into Real Estate and not have to get a second job to pay it off. My husband already works two jobs.

Does anyone know the laws in Washington State governing out of state purchases, companies doing business from other states, in home sales and all that? If they do I'd love to hear from them.

Someone please contact me about how to handle the credit card company. Unfortunately for me, we transferred the outstanding balance to a lower interest card."

Further research led us to the Revised Code of Washington. In Chapter 19.110 RCW of the Washington Business Opportunity Fraud Act were the updated Federal and State laws. This could be accessed at findlaw.com. The entire text is about 12 pages long. These can be found in the "For Legal Professionals" section. This website also has a "For the Public" section with a lot of resources. This site is free and you do not have to be a legal professional to access any area of this site. There are no ads or pop-ups.

Here are some highlights of the Washington Business Opportunity Fraud Act:

RCW 19.110.020
Definitions.
Unless the context clearly requires otherwise, the definitions in this section apply throughout this chapter.

(1) "Business opportunity" means the sale or lease of any product, equipment, supply, or service which is sold or leased to enable the purchaser to start a business; and:

(a) The seller represents that the seller will provide locations or assist the purchaser in finding locations, on premises neither owned nor leased by the purchaser or seller, for the use or operation of vending machines, display racks, cases, or similar devices or coin-operated amusement machines or similar devices; or

(b) The seller represents that the seller will purchase any product made, produced, fabricated, assembled, modified, grown, or bred by the purchaser using, in whole or part, any product, equipment, supply, or service sold or leased to the purchaser by the seller; or

(c) The seller guarantees that the purchaser will earn an income greater than or equal to the price paid for the business opportunity; or

(d) The seller represents that if the purchaser pays a fee exceeding three hundred dollars directly or indirectly for the purpose of the seller providing a sales or marketing program, the seller will provide such a program which will enable the purchaser to derive income from the business opportunity which exceeds the price paid for the business opportunity.

(2) "Person" includes an individual, corporation, partnership, joint venture, or any business entity.

(3) "Seller" means a person who sells or leases a business opportunity.

(4) "Purchaser" means a person who buys or leases a business opportunity.

(5) "Director" means the director of financial institutions.

(6) "Guarantee" means an undertaking by the seller to refund all or a portion of the purchase price paid for the business opportunity.

RCW 19.110.030
Sale or lease of business opportunity—Offer to sell or lease business opportunity—Occurrence in Washington.

(1) An offer to sell or offer to lease a business opportunity occurs in Washington when:

(a) The offer is made in Washington; or

(b) The purchaser resides in Washington at the time of the offer and the business opportunity is or will be located, in whole or in part, in the state of Washington; or

(c) The offer originates from Washington; or

(d) The business opportunity is or will be, in whole or in part, located in Washington.

(2) An offer does not occur in Washington if a seller advertises only in a newspaper having more than two-thirds of its circulation outside the state of Washington, or on a radio or television program originating outside the state and does not sell or lease business opportunities in Washington.

(3) A sale or lease of a business opportunity occurs in Washington when:

(a) The sale or lease is made in Washington; or

(b) The purchaser resides in Washington at the time of the sale or lease, and the business opportunity is or will be located, in whole or in part, in Washington; or

(c) The business opportunity is or will be located in Washington.

You may also be interested in Chapter 19.190 RCW COMMERCIAL ELECTRONIC MAIL. This Chapter includes, but is not limited to:

19.190.020 Unpermitted or misleading electronic mail—Prohibition.
19.190.030 Unpermitted or misleading electronic mail—Violation of consumer protection act.
19.190.040 Violations—Damages.

Please read the following sections of the Code of Federal Regulations in regards to deceptive telemarketing and abusive telemarketing (CFR).

16 CFR Ch. I (1-1-05 Edition)

§ 310.3 Deceptive telemarketing acts or practices

and

§ 310.4 Abusive telemarketing acts or practices.

Highlights:

§ 310.3
(a) Prohibited deceptive telemarketing acts or practices. It is a deceptive telemarketing act or practice and a violation of this Rule for any seller or telemarketer to engage in the following conduct:

(1) Before a customer pays for goods or services offered,

failing to disclose truthfully, in a clear and conspicuous manner, the following material information:

(i) The total costs to purchase, receive, or use, and the quantity of, any goods or services that are the subject of the sales offer;

(ii) All material restrictions, limitations, or conditions to purchase, receive, or use the goods or services that are the subject of the sales offer;

(iii) If the seller has a policy of not making refunds, cancellations, exchanges, or repurchases, a statement informing the customer that this is the seller's policy; or, if the seller or telemarketer makes a representation about a refund, cancellation, exchange, or repurchase policy, a statement of all material terms and conditions of such policy; . . .

(2) Misrepresenting, directly or by implication, in the sale of goods or services any of the following material information:

(i) The total costs to purchase, receive, or use, and the quantity of, any goods or services that are the subject of a sales offer;

(ii) Any material restriction, limitation, or condition to purchase, receive, or use goods or services that are the subject of a sales offer;

(iii) Any material aspect of the performance, efficacy, nature, or central characteristics of goods or services that are the subject of a sales offer;

(iv) Any material aspect of the nature or terms of the seller's refund, cancellation, exchange, or repurchase policies; . . .

(vi) Any material aspect of an investment opportunity including, but not limited to, risk, liquidity, earnings potential, or profitability;

. . .

Here is some more information on "Design-a-Site" and how to file a complaint with State of Utah!

A little bit of further info, in case it helps any of who have been ripped off.

#1—
Doing a 'whois' search on the domains "Design-a-Site" Mentors shows that both belong to:

Registrant:
xxxxxxxx
xxxxxxxx

The technical contact for both domains shows a domain of _____

Try _____ and you'll find what looks like another get-rich-quick scam with _____ listed.

Hope this helps anybody researching "Design-a-Site". They all seem to be the same company according to these domain registrations.

You can check it yourself by going to any "whois lookup" website such as http://whois.godaddy.com

#2—
If the contracts that you've signed with "Design-a-Site" or any of their other names are not in compliance with Utah state law regarding sales of business opportunities then you can file a complaint with the Utah Department of Commerce's Division of Consumer Protection. Even though the companies say they're selling educational products and services, it sounds like from what y'all are saying that their sales guys

are pushing a business opportunity through high pressure tactics.

So here are links to the business opportunity laws and the complaint form:

* http://www.commerce.utah.gov/dcp/en . . . nt/ statute.html
* http://www.le.state.ut.us/~code/TITLE13/13_12.html
Specifically click links to read sections 13-15-4 and 13-15-5.

If you feel you've been misled then the right thing to do is to file a complaint, no matter how long ago it was, in order to protect the public
* *http://www.commerce.utah.gov/dcp/en . . ./complaint. html*

It was amazing to me to see how many laws were being broken by this company. Where were the people who were supposed to be enforcing these laws? My only wish was that I could have known this information prior to purchasing the Web builder.

It baffles me that there is so much information on the Internet. Hopefully, the experience and the research can act as a training tool for anyone who is looking to venture into an Internet experience.

Chapter 2

Prelude to Nykaos4u

*O*nce most of my items and pictures were uploaded, I opened the Web site. New suppliers were being added weekly. Then the first message came . . .

"I'm going to stalk you," he said. My initial reaction to this statement was that this was probably someone I knew trying to play a joke on me. Once the conversation continued, I realized that I was wrong.

"Girls are *scaredy* cat's and they believe everything on the news. They always have to feel safe. Don't they?

"Women don't like it when they don't have control." Then he continued to go on about the rape statistics. At this point in time, I realized that this was nobody that I knew. No one that I know would say any such thing.

After contemplating what I could do, I decided to close out my Yahoo! account. Were they watching my moves through Yahoo! or was it my computer? I needed to try to figure it out. A few minutes later, I reopened a new account. As I continued to upload pictures to my Web site, now I had two different usernames start to message me. After spending several minutes answering the questions, I realized that the two were the same person. They were both asking me the same questions just slightly reworded. So I stopped talking to the one and continued with the other. By the end of the conversation, I told the guy that I did not have time for his nonsense but was going to bed. Logging off under my newly created Natalie username, I then logged on under my neighbor's account, Lisa. No sooner did I log on when someone else began to message me and say, "I thought you were going to bed."

"That was Natalie this is Lisa. How the hell are you doing this? Now you have really pissed me off!"

Then later on in the chat, they said they knew who I was and where I lived. Wishing that this was a joke, I made the comment "yeah right." At this point, he proceeded to type my name and address.

My stomach began to shake and tighten up. My worst nightmare just came true. This threat was for real! After dismissing earlier ideas that this was a prank during the first chat when I realized that none of my real friends or associates would threaten me and make the comments that were made to me. They really knew who I was and where I lived.

Now my heart began to beat like it was coming out of my chest. Who were these people? Were they really stalking me? Was my ex-husband playing a joke on me, or was he really mad at me? What were they going to do to me? Would I disappear? Would I be killed? Now all of the possible scenarios began to run through my head.

Immediately, I called the New York State police department. It did not bother me that it was already early in the morning, about 3:00 AM. I knew it would take some time for them to show up since I live in the country and was about twenty-plus minutes from the State Troopers barracks.

I returned to the computer. I had saved the chat in a Word document. By the time I printed the chat, it had already been altered. It still contained the threats including my name and address.

A short while later, two policemen showed up. I explained to them that I thought my identity had been stolen and that my life was in danger. After going into detail about what happened, I completed a police report. They told me that they did not think that they could get to my case for at least three months. "Homicides take precedence," they said.

Responding quickly, I said, "Don't you think that is backwards? You mean to tell me that I have to become a statistic, which would mean that I was dead before you even get to my case? Well then, I will have to make sure they leave a long trail so that if anything happens to me, you will find out who did it."

"We are not very well versed in computer crimes. This is a new field for us. However, we will forward your information to our newly created New York State Internet crime division for further investigation."

"Computers are a new field for me too. I am not sure how they are doing this or why, but I will find out. I really don't want to become a statistic, a dead one at that."

"We will have them contact you shortly."

Needless to say, I did not get much sleep that night. I kept on going over what had happened in my head. It made me feel unsafe and violated. If something happened to me, would anyone even know where I was or whom I was with or what happened to me? I could disappear, be tortured or worse yet, end up dead. The threats they made were not taken lightly. They are words that I will never repeat. I will not even acknowledge them by placing their chat in this book.

The next day I was contacted by Investigator Paul of the New York State Internet crime division. He was very concerned about what had happened. When I explained that I thought my identity was stolen, he seemed to believe me. He asked me if I had noticed anything strange that had happened in my life in the past few months. However, when I explained my gut feeling that these guys were targeting me from three possible scenarios, he looked confused.

The first scenario I mentioned was that I had been going through a nasty divorce. I had mentioned that it was possible that my ex-husband could be behind it. Although he had no computer experience, he had the means and the people at his disposal to do so.

One specific event came into my memory. Back in February of 2003, I had received a phone call from my ex-husband. Once our separation and divorce were finalized, I had only spoken to him on five occasions. Every time we had spoken, it was not pleasant. On two of the occasions, he had threatened to force the sale of the house. We had a joint mortgage on our house. In our divorce agreement, I had agreed to get the house remortgaged or have his name removed from the existing mortgage. Under a three-year deadline to have his name removed, I was able to get his name off it in less than a year. Being two years ahead of the deadline allowed me to go ahead with the porch repairs.

When seeing the porch ripped off the house, he called me up to complain that he was not able to move ahead in his life since he was still on the mortgage. He said that he was going to force the sale of the house. At this point in time, I informed him that I had already had him removed from the existing mortgage. I explained that he contact his attorney in order to have her contact my attorney. All that he needed to do was to submit a letter to the credit agencies with a letter from the bank that removed him as payee on the loan. After making this suggestion, I did not hear anything for several weeks.

Upon completion of the wraparound porch, of which I was able to incorporate a gazebo into the corner, he had called me up to complain. Once again, he threatened to force the sale of the house. He said that the mortgage was still showing up on his credit report. Once again, I said that he should have his attorney contact my attorney. All that was required was for his attorney to send the credit agencies the updated information. The mortgage would remain on his credit report, but it would show that he had no balance or responsibility for the remaining loan. The house was the only thing his name was still attached to that we had shared together when we were married. He had a hard time accepting that he no longer had any control over me once I had his name removed from the mortgage. The control was finally severed!

Now back to the February 2003 phone call that came out of the blue. He told me that he and his girlfriend were going to sell their house and be moving down south to Virginia where her family was from. He did not want me to hear it on the street. He thought that mentioning the move to me directly would be the "right thing to do." I told him that I knew that he always wanted to move south and wished him the best.

Then he said something that I will never forget. He said that he had heard that I "got one hell of an attorney." It was at this point that I realized that he had information that only one other person in my life had, my mother. However, I knew that she would not even talk to him. I was only in the process of changing attorneys. I had not even finalized my decision yet. The only other way he could have known about that would have been if he had read my e-mail correspondence with my potential new attorney. At this point, although I suspected that my e-mail was being tampered with, I could not prove anything. So I tabled my thoughts.

Piecing together his previous comments, I figured this phone call was out of line for him. He was rather pleasant and not argumentative for once. Perhaps he wanted me to confirm his suspicions, which I would not even confirm or deny.

He also had another reason for possibly having my personal identity stolen. After first separating, he told me, "No one ever leaves me. If you ever attempt to, they would never find your body. Without a body, I could never be prosecuted." I knew that remaining silent on such a threat would not keep me safe. Taking steps to protect myself, I hired a private investigator. Protecting my life was of prime importance and concern to me. Months later, when he had found out that someone had been watching him, he made the comment "No one ever does that to me and gets away with it. Payback's a bitch!"

Now I find out my computer is hacked. They are threatening me and stealing my identity. The thought crossed my mind that it was possible that he might be behind the hacking. Not that he could do that himself, but he had the money and means to have that done. That was one scenario.

Now there was a second. In early February, I had received a computer virus in my e-mail again. This was the second time in less than three months. Once again I had telephoned my local computer repair guy, Gary. This was my first computer guy and not the one who was referred to me by my neighbor. After being told that he could not just simply fix the computer, he told me he had to wipe the hard drive and reinstall the operating system. He took my computer home to repair. After paying him much more to repair the computer than I had originally figured, I was back in operation. It was not until several weeks into the investigation that I found out that he had installed the original Trojan and Keylogger, which led to the hackers from New York and New Jersey gaining access to my computer.

Then the third possibility could be that it was just a random act of criminal activity.

However, there was another incident that happened. Earlier in the year, I had received a phone call from my own electric company. Mike was the man on the other end of the phone. He told me that they had not received my payment on my electric account. Supposedly, I was now three months in arrears. After mentioning to him that I had sent a check out a few weeks previous, I asked to him to research the payment that had not posted to my account. A few minutes later, he informed me that he could not locate that check. I told him that I wanted to call my bank to see if the check had cleared and asked him if I could call back. He informed me that if I did not make payment arrangements before I hung up, my electric would be turned off the next day. After expressing my concern that perhaps my check had cleared my bank and was posted to the wrong account, I did not want to make an additional payment if it was not necessary. However, I did not want the electric to be turned off. So I agreed to make a payment through my checking account over the phone. After telling him how much I wanted to pay, he made the comment, "Are you sure that you have enough funds in your checking account to cover this?"

Immediately I knew something was wrong. I asked for his name, employee identification number, and phone number to return his call once I verified with my bank what happened to the check. Any bill collector that I have ever dealt with has never made a statement like that before.

My first phone call was to my bank. After giving them my account number, they tried to pull it up. It was at this horrifying point that they told me my account had been closed for the past week. In the meantime, I had been writing out checks against a closed account. No one from the bank had even notified me of what happened. At this point, a panic set in. Not only did they close my bank account, but they used my line of credit to the tune of seven hundred dollars! I told them about the phone call that I had just received.

Immediately, I drove to the bank to open up a new account. After gathering any evidence that the bank had, I filed a police report.

Upon returning home, I phoned my electric company. I called a phone number that was listed on my bill. Giving them the name and the employee identification number that was given to me, they were able to verify that this employee did in fact work for them. When I asked to speak to him, I was told that he was out today. However, I had spoken to someone some time earlier in the day. After he had made the statement that he did, my gut told me that I was not dealing with the electric company. Thank goodness I had not given him my bank account information. After reviewing the events in my head, I felt like he already had this information. How could someone have closed my bank account? How could an employee of my electric company know that I was having trouble with my bank account when I did not even know what had happened?

The investigator's mind began to reel over the possibilities. He reiterated that it would be several months before they could get to my case. I was in the middle of opening up an Internet store and needed the computer. What to do!

Although I had expected my e-mail had been hacked a few months earlier, I had other reasons to believe that my identity had been stolen. I was in the process of opening an online Internet store selling dance clothing, equipment, and accessories. While I was uploading the pictures, the first message was sent to me. My initial thought was that someone I knew was playing a prank on me. It was not until they said that "women don't like it when they don't have control" and then they went on about the rape statistics that I realized my real friends would never play a joke like this on me. Then they said, "We are stalking you." At this point in time, a nauseating feeling came over me. My stomach became tied up in knots and began to shake. Reliving the previous night's events upset me even more. It was that same feeling you get when you are forced to do something that you are not ready to handle. Usually a victim goes into one mode; either it is *flight* or *fight*. Either choice is frightening to make. The unknown usually has the power to make you feel that way. Since the flight method was going to get me nowhere, I decided to stand my ground and fight to reclaim my identity. It is amazing how one letter can make such a difference in a word. Flight or fight equals fright to most people, but not me. My equation is flight and fight equals freedom, freedom from the lies, deceit, terror, and even death.

Now I went into survival mode. I needed to figure out at least one of the hackers' identities. Since they already knew who I was and where I lived, I decided to make them leave a long trail of evidence in my computer. After changing my identity twice that first night, I realized that I could not hide from them. Instead, I got angry and wanted justice.

Since the two previous conversations were with the same person, I could not tell if they were in my computer or in Yahoo! When I had logged on under my neighbor's name, he continued to talk to me. All of the usernames involved so far said that they had seen me in a chat room. Since I do not go into chat rooms, I knew that it was not me. Either someone had hacked Yahoo! my account, or they were in my computer.

How could someone be accessing my computer with a firewall and antivirus program operating? I opened my firewall control panel and noticed that my settings had been changed. Changing them back to what they should be set at, I resumed my work.

Shortly later, I checked the settings of my firewall. Once again, the settings had been changed. How could someone be doing this while I was working on my computer? This time, I opened the settings on my desktop and continued to watch them. To my surprise, the settings were changed in front of my eyes. I quickly pulled out my camcorder and filmed my computer screen.

Later that day, my neighbor stopped in for a visit. I told her that she would not believe what was going on. Changing the settings in my firewall back again, we continued to watch my computer. A few minutes later, the settings were changed. Neither one of us was near the computer or the mouse. Somehow, the computer was being controlled from the background.

"Wow, someone is hacked in your computer. I know someone who can help you figure out who it is," she said.

When she returned home, she called me. She gave me her father's name and number. He supposedly was a computer wizard. The only problem was he was living in Florida. With computers, I guess there is no need to be nearby since my computer was already being controlled by someone else.

Once I received his phone number, I called him. Unfortunately, he was not home. However, I left a message with my number for him to return the phone call.

Later that evening, I received a phone call from Hack::, who was visiting a friend of his in Virginia. After explaining who I was and that I received his phone number from his daughter, I explained my dilemma.

I had spent several weeks setting up my new Web site. How could I operate and receive orders on my computer knowing that someone had gained access to it? Although all orders were being placed through a secure Web site, whoever was in my computer could view everything that I could see. Since the back end of my shopping cart gave me access to view all credit information including name, address, phone number, credit card number, expiration date, and amount, the hacker would also be able to see this data.

Expressing my new concerns to the police, I started to research my options. I could not understand how the program for the shopping cart that I was using would record all of this data. Even though orders were being placed through a secure Web site, my computer was not secure. Although I had taken many precautions by installing a firewall, antivirus program, and hardware firewall, someone had found a way to bypass all of it. Whatever I could view on my computer, the hacker could also see. I believed that I was being targeted by hackers because they were interested in stealing credit information of my customers.

In the meantime, I decided to talk to one of the technicians at Coyote Cable Connections the following day. Perhaps someone could show me how this could be done through Yahoo! I thought that by learning Yahoo! better, then I could understand how this could be done. I googled the phrase "hacking Yahoo!" I was directed to a Web site that gave instructions on how to steal a person's Yahoo! account. Upon further investigation, the new version of Yahoo! prevented the directions from working. I was curious to know how someone had gained access to my Yahoo! accounts. Some of my accounts were hijacked completely, and I never got them back.

After phoning Coyote Cable Connections, I explained my dilemma to one of the technicians. I had expressed concern that my e-mail account had also been compromised. The technician gave me the name of someone that he thought could help me with the Yahoo! issue. This was someone who had worked at Coyote Cable Connections in the past according to the technician.

We spoke through Yahoo! instant messaging at first. He then gave me his number to call. Using a calling card, I phoned him. Once again not knowing if he was involved with the hackers, I did not want my home phone to show up on his caller ID. Once I felt assured of his answers, we set up a time to meet.

My neighbor made plans to be here with me when he came. He was going to install a program that would prevent me from getting booted from Yahoo! which was a big problem. Knowing that my computer was not secure, it did not bother me to have this done. The police were all aware of what was going on.

He showed up at the house to work on the computer. He installed the program to help prevent me from getting booted. While there, he accessed his e-mail account. He had had someone's username and password e-mailed to him. He then accessed the Yahoo! account and changed the password and answers to the questions so that the original owner of the Yahoo! account could no longer access their account. I found it interesting that he used my computer and my IP address to do this. If and when it became necessary to see where the change of information occurred, then it would show my IP address.

Thankfully, I had several eyewitnesses that observed what had happened. It was at this moment that I realized I could not trust him. He left shortly after that.

The next day, I received an instant message from him. While in chat with him, I mentioned that I did not like the fact that he hijacked someone else's account from my computer. Before I told him this, I had changed my password on my main account but did not have a chance to change it on the other account. When I mentioned that I did not think that it was a good idea to keep talking, he tried to boot me. He was unsuccessful in booting me. However, I was in chat with the police officer. Shortly after, I received a phone call from Investigator Paul.

"That son of a . . . booted me! Not only did he boot me, but he hijacked my account!

"He flooded my Yahoo! Whatever he did to you, I believe, was meant for me. I need to check my other Yahoo! account and change the password . . . It's not letting me in. He must have hijacked that account.

"No one has ever been so brazen to do that to me. He will not get away with this.

Finally, something happened to get the police more interested in my case. This could be a good thing for me. Now the hackers have their attention. Maybe now they will take the case more seriously.

The following day, I phoned the guy at Coyote Cable Connections to tell him what happened. When I told him that his friend contacted me, he asked me how I made out. I told him his friend was a hacker and had hijacked my Yahoo! account. He said that his friend would never have done that. He asked me for his name. After telling him, he adamantly denied even knowing him. Now I did not know what to believe. It was not until I met my computer guy that I would learn of the true relationship between the employee of Coyote Cable Connections and one of the hackers.

Chapter 3

Piecing the Crimes Together

*N*ot having any computer instruction or degree at this point in time, I needed to rule out one of the two options. This is where my "street smarts" needed to come in. As I continued to upload my pictures and item descriptions to my Web site, different identities continued to message me. There was one in particular that caught my attention, mandel1410305. After a few conversations by instant message, I told him that if he wanted to continue to speak with me online, then I wanted to hear his voice over the phone. I used a calling card to make this call. Just in case he was not the hacker, I did not want him to know who I was or where I lived. The 800 number on the calling card would display on a caller ID instead of my home number. After a brief conversation, I hung up. Now I had a phone number with a user ID.

How could I know that the person on the other end of the instant message was the same name and phone number of the person that I was speaking to on the phone?

I needed to get him to turn on his webcam to see his picture. Before I could do that, I found a free program on the Internet so that I could snag a picture of my desktop. After installing the program on my computer, I tested it out. Now the trick would be to get him to turn on his webcam for me. He had denied my viewing his webcam on previous occasions. He told me that he did not have a webcam. However, Yahoo! showed the webcam icon next to his username.

My real friends from Oregon called me a few days later. She told me that someone had been messaging her. After telling me who, I told her that I thought that he was one of the hackers. I suggested not speaking with him at all. She told me that she would continue to talk to him and pass any important information from the chats to me. I taught her the trick that the New York State Internet crime division taught me.

> Select Start
> All Programs
> Accessories
> Command Prompt
> Type *netstat—an*

This will give her the IP address of the computer that is connected to the username that she is in chat with. However, if she could get him to turn on his webcam, then she could snag the direct IP address since he would have a direct connection to her computer. She told me that he had turned on his webcam for her on numerous occasions. It should not be a problem to get him to turn it on again. After giving her the name of the free program to snag a copy of her desktop, she agreed to forward me his picture. She also agreed that upon completion of the chats, she would e-mail me the chats and the IP addresses. After she told me that he had turned on his webcam for her, I came up with a plan.

I purchased a webcam and installed it on my computer. Aiming it at the curtain in my room, I went online as my friend, under her username. He requested to view the webcam, but I denied him.

"You denying me?" he said.

"Not until you turn yours on," I replied.

As soon as he turned on his webcam, I snagged his picture. After printing the picture in color, he then requested to view my webcam. He thought that he was speaking to my friends from Oregon. When I turned on my cam, he started to curse and swear since I had tricked him into turning on his webcam for me.

"Oh, it's you!" he wrote.

"If we are going to continue to speak with each other, I need to know a little more about you. Why did you lie to me about not having a webcam?" I inquired.

"With all of the trouble that you are having with your computer, I did not want them to hassle me," he said.

"You must understand that I need to know about you if you would like to continue to speak with me," I replied.

"You have nothing to worry about with me."

"I know that you are not involved. The police are on the case and I am not that concerned just a little cautious. After only speaking with you for a few weeks, I still feel like I don't know you."

Needing for him to believe that I did not think he was involved in the hacking was essential to gain his trust. After all, I had exposed his identity to me through his webcam. However, how do I know if the person I am viewing is the same person that is chatting with me by instant message and the same person on the other end of the phone? People can hide behind a computer. They can make it appear that they are someone else.

After doing some research on the Internet, I realized it was possible for someone to upload someone else's picture. Someone must have been logging into my account and entering into a chat room. Perhaps someone I knew was playing a joke on me. After seeing his picture, I knew that I did not know who it was. Now all I needed to do was to confirm that the person on the other end of the instant message matched the picture and the voice on the other end of the phone. I decided to get him to turn on his webcam once more. While viewing him on my computer, I then called him and watched him answer the phone. Bingo! Now I knew that the person I was viewing was the same person on the end of the phone. I did a reverse lookup of the phone number on switchboard.com and got his full name and address. However, when dealing with hackers, how would I know whether he was using his real name or had stolen someone else's identity?

Sometime later, I messaged him from work. He explained to me that he did not want me to chat with him from my home computer.

He feared that they were trying to gain access to his computer. He stated his concern that Yahoo! had been hacked and that his account was being affected as well. However, the Yahoo! hack was not public information until a few weeks later. Either he was one of the hackers or he had association with one of them.

My previous experience with the hacker whose claim to fame was "how many Yahoo! accounts he hijacked" taught me that someone could have an unlimited number of usernames. He had showed me how he could log into a chat room under almost fifty names. In other words, he could be the only one in a chat room. He said he liked messing with women's heads. He would talk to them from different identities. One identity would accuse her of talking to others in the chat room. Another identity would be businesslike. Yet another identity would be nasty. In other words, you would not know that you were talking to the same person but under different identities.

On one occasion, I had been communicating through Yahoo! from my part-time job. After reassuring him that I would only communicate to him by instant message from work, we agreed to talk the next day. As planned, I logged online in Yahoo! during my break time. As soon as he saw that I was online, he began to message me. Once again, he brought up his concerns about his computer. He said that he was having numerous problems with it and thought that whoever had hacked my computer was messing with his. After reassuring him that I had a suspicion of who was behind it, I diverted his attention to another username. This person was the only one who was in contact with both of us. After becoming aware that this person had multiple usernames, I suspected him as well. Trying to convince him that I knew he was not involved in the hacking, I had led him to believe that I would talk to him the following day from work. Neglecting to tell him that I would be at home, I proceeded to message him. After several minutes, I received a message from him asking me if I was home today. He would not have known that I was home unless he was monitoring my computer. Perhaps by making him believe that I was at work, I could distinguish whether or not he was monitoring my computer. After all, the hackers were not too smart. Tricking one of the hackers into turning his webcam on for me exposed one identity to me. At least I had a face to go with the username, phone number, name, and address.

The following day I messaged him as if I was at work. The conversation continued for a short time. Then about five minutes into the conversation, he said, "Are you at home today?" I told him no. That was the last thing he said to me that day. He would not have known that I was home unless he was monitoring my computer. Now I knew that he was viewing my computer.

Now I had a new concern. Since they now had control of my computer, would they be able to gain access to my webcam to further spy on me? When I booted my computer, I noticed that the light on the webcam would come on and then go off. Not knowing if this was normal, I decided to err on the side of caution. Feeling as if my privacy was being invaded, I kept it unplugged when it was not in use. The webcam had a microphone built into it. I did not want anyone seeing or hearing anything going on in the privacy of my own home. Eavesdropping and spying on someone without the consent of the other party whether written or oral is illegal. All I knew was that these guys had to be making a living all off what they were doing. They were online most of the evening and into the wee hours of the morning.

Chapter 4

The Rendezvous

*T*he events in my life as well as the media news events began to piece together like a puzzle. Before my new computer guy would make the trip to New York, he was going to send his best friend to my home to retrieve the data and reformat my computer. Once he could sense the severity and extent of the problem, then he would schedule a trip up here.

He arranged for his friend to come up to make a ghost copy of my hard drive. A ghost copy of the hard drive would allow the police to replicate my computer. It would include all the files that were on my hard drive. In other words, it would contain all the evidence the police would need in order to convict those who had hacked my computer. By installing the CDs on a formatted computer, this would allow the police to retrieve all the proof they needed.

However, the first thing on the agenda was to retrieve the information off my computer. The police had me back up the chats, Word documents, pictures, and programs. There was a Word document containing altered chats that had been placed in one of my folders in my documents. These chats were placed in my computer to scare me off from turning my computer over to the police. However, their plan backfired. I explained what I found and why I thought they were placed there. I told him not to be shocked at the content in the altered chats. He told me that nothing would surprise him.

Once a full copy of my hard drive was burned to eight CDs, my computer was then reformatted so that I could continue to build my Web site. Then I would not have to turn my computer over to the police, who said that they could not get to my case for three months, but the ghost copy could be used to redo my computer to retrieve the information on how, why, and when the hackers got into my computer. He was given some government programs to install in order to help track the hackers and their activities.

Upon the CDs being successfully burned, they were then turned over to the New York State Internet crime division. The procedure to replicate my computer began. However, during the installation, one of the CDs was not able to be opened. If it's not one thing, it's another.

After explaining to my new computer guy what had happened, he suggested forwarding the CDs to him. He had a program that was able to retrieve all the data from the corrupted CD. He then created a new computer with all the data from my previously hacked computer. He was able to retrieve all the data from all of the CDs. There were log files that also documented where, when, and who had placed the altered documents into my computer. For once, a sense of relief came over me. Finally, there was a way to prove what had happened! Did you realize that even a computer that was in a fire, the data can be reproduced? Did you realize that anything that is erased from a hard drive can be retrieved? There are log files that track every keystroke on a computer. An infected computer such as mine contains many additional copies.

When Windows was reinstalled on my computer, before I even went online, a Keylogger and Trojan were found on my computer. That meant the Windows program that my previous computer guy had installed and given me a copy of was corrupt. A new version of Windows was then installed. The antivirus program and firewall were then installed.

We phoned my Internet provider to have them reassign me an IP address. This way it would be as though I were someone new who was first accessing the Internet.

However, within a few minutes, my computer got hit with a Keylogger and Trojan. Only Coyote Cable Connections was allowed to bypass my firewall. It seemed that somehow the hacker was working through the cable company or someone at the company itself was behind it.

After uninstalling the Trojan and Keylogger, we repeated the process. The same thing continued to happen repeatedly. Finally, we spoke to someone else at Coyote Cable Connections. We explained the problems we were having accessing the Internet. We believed the Trojan and Keylogger were coming through the Coyote Cable Connections server. They reassigned our access point. Then it seemed to be all right.

Now with all this happening, I was starting to believe that Coyote Cable Connections was in on it. I still was not sure if my computer was the only thing hacked or if, in fact, Yahoo! had been hacked. My conversations with Mandel led me to believe that Yahoo! had been hacked. When I googled the news story, it did not show up. Since some time had passed when I had learned of the hacking, I did a new search. This time, the story came up on the Internet. Researching back into the copies of the chats, I realized that "Mandel" had told me of the news several weeks before it became public. Perhaps he was behind the hack of Yahoo! himself. How else could he have known about the hack in advance? The only other way he could have known would have been if he knew who the hacker was or if he did it himself.

Once we were able to access the Internet without getting bombed with Trojans and Keyloggers, we finished installing all the other programs that I needed for my Web site design and tracking the hackers. All of the other installations seemed to go without a hitch. My computer was now secure to access the Internet. I set up Yahoo! again as well as AOL account this time. A new identity gave me a feeling of added safety, but I still felt guarded. Once my computer was secured, plans were then made for my new computer guy to make a visit once the snow finished melting.

It was an unusually warm spring day of 2003. Seeing the green grass was very welcoming to the eyes. The air had that hint of freshness making you long for the end of the winter. Winters in this area are usually long, harsh, and cold.

I had arranged for my neighbor's father, who was a computer guru, to show up at my house. While sitting outside on my newly renovated wraparound porch, a blue Mustang pulled up into my driveway. It was Hack. He had traveled from Florida for a visit to assess my computer problems.

After several minutes of introductions, we sat down at the round glass table on the porch. With a glass of iced tea in one hand and my paperwork in the other, I proceeded to the table. After relating to him how I figured out the first hacker's identity, I proceeded to show him the picture of Mandel that I had snagged from his webcam.

"Is this a joke?" he screamed.

"No, why would you think that?"

"This is a joke. How could you know?"

"Know what?"

"I know who this is."

"How do you know this guy?"

"I thought this guy was some lowlife that I had dealt with in the past. He was blackmailing a friend of mine, lollybug. She was having an Internet affair with some guy in California. He secretly taped her webcam sessions with her boyfriend. He then tried to get her to pay a large sum of money in exchange for the tapes so that her husband would never see them. She hired me to track down this guy. At that time, he tried to hack my computer, but instead, I hacked his. I fried his machine, motherboard and all."

"No way!"

"Yes way!"

"How long ago did this happen?"

"It was at least three years ago if not longer."

"Well, I guess he still is up to his old tricks. As I had told you on the phone, I believe he is accessing people's computers and webcams without their permission. He is online most of the night. I believe he is making money all off the crimes he is committing. I believe my webcam was being accessed and that the video was being uploaded to the Internet. I know my computer was hacked. I know they were and still are accessing the back end of my shopping cart on my Web site. They can view people's names, addresses, credit card numbers, and expiration dates. If this guy is the same person who was blackmailing your friend with webcam tapes, then I believe he has not stopped. He supposedly is a stockbroker. He works on spreadsheets all night long. However, the spreadsheets that he is working on, I believe, are those used to make movies and videos."

"I had no idea that this guy was still in business. I thought that what happened was a once in a lifetime event, possibly someone who was hired by someone else."

"What are the possibilities? Who would have known that I would have met the computer guy who originally put him out of business! What are the odds?"

"I really thought this was a joke. How did you get his picture?"

After showing him the chats, he laughed. "I guess he picked the wrong computer to hack. Believe me; I will make sure he is put out of business permanently." Then he continued, "I can't believe this! This is so unbelievable."

"Well, here is his name, address, and phone number."

"Wow! Somebody did their homework. I see he is still at the same address that he was three years ago."

"I am still shocked that you know him. Of all the people in this world, how was I directed to meet you, the same person who crossed paths with this guy in the past?"

My computer guy and I came up with a plan. We decided to create two user accounts. They would both contain a username of two previous victims of these hackers. Sasha and lollybug were the names. Since my computer guy was familiar with both of these women, he decided to play a trick on them. He logged on as sasha and I logged on as lollybug. However, lollybug's profile contained sasha's personal information and sasha's profile contained lollybug's picture and personal information. While on the phone with my computer guy, we decided to follow rocknrollforever into a chat room. My computer guy told me what to type in the chat. Although I believed that Mandel was behind the hacking, my gut was telling me that this guy was the head honcho.

Lollybug proceeded to chat with him. Since my computer guy was familiar with the way she spoke, he had me type phrases, names, and words that she had used with him in the past. He had turned on his webcam to view. He told me what to say. Here is the chat.

rocknrollforever:	well hello there
lollybug3369:	hello
rocknrollforever:	so, what brings you in here
lollybug3369:	you dear
rocknrollforever:	is that so . . . .
lollybug3369:	yes i remember you well
lollybug3369:	you remember me?
rocknrollforever:	we havent hooked up yet . . . . still want to ?
rocknrollforever:	ignoring me now ?!?!
lollybug3369:	you did not answer my question. do you remember me sweetie?
rocknrollforever:	i believe i do
rocknrollforever:	but you changed your name
lollybug3369:	who are you talking about?
rocknrollforever:	i dont know . . . i recall a woman i use to chat with from northern pa . . . is that you ?
lollybug3369:	who do you think i am?
rocknrollforever:	cant remember your name
lollybug3369:	when was the last time you spoke to me?
rocknrollforever:	over a year
lollybug3369:	try 5 years
rocknrollforever:	that long ?
lollybug3369:	at least

lollybug3369:   still up to your old tricks?

rocknrollforever: that depends

lollybug3369:   on what?

rocknrollforever: yes, i am still looking for fun . . . are you

rocknrollforever's status is now "View My Webcam" (1/9/2004 12:00 PM)

lollybug3369:   after all you guys put me through, do you honestly think

rocknrollforever: what guys ?

lollybug3369:   you know who

lollybug3369:   just remember payback is a BITCH

rocknrollforever: hmmmm, now you have me lost

lollybug3369:   you will find out soon enough.

rocknrollforever: hmmm, i guess i dont really know who you are then

lollybug3369:   yes you do

lollybug3369:   but i have changed thanks to you

rocknrollforever: well, i think you have me confused with someone else then

lollybug3369:   well what is your name?

rocknrollforever: you tell me if you think you know me silly

lollybug3369:   ok mike

lollybug3369:   am i right?

rocknrollforever: yep

rocknrollforever: and you are ?

lollybug3369:   lolly

lollybug3369:   Laurie

lollybug3369:   what?

lollybug3369:   you don't remember me?

rocknrollforever: from where ?

lollybug3369:   PA

rocknrollforever: i know . . . where in pa

lollybug3369: i do not hand out that info on here. you should know that.

rocknrollforever: why are you mad at me ?

lollybug3369: I never said I was mad.

rocknrollforever: . . . now you have me confused

lollybug3369: I just like messing with your head.

lollybug3369: It is fun

rocknrollforever: so, you still wanna meet up with me then ?

lollybug3369: I never said that.

rocknrollforever: haha, so thats a no then

rocknrollforever: man

lollybug3369: man what?

rocknrollforever: where is your pic ?

lollybug3369: i do not have one now.

lollybug3369: i see you still have an old pic posted.

rocknrollforever: not that old

lollybug3369: how old?

rocknrollforever: less then a year

lollybug3369: you must still have some video floating around.

rocknrollforever: video ?

lollybug3369: do you speak english? that is what I said.

lollybug3369: visit my friends profile and take a look at my pic

rocknrollforever: and that is ?

lollybug3369: http://profiles.yahoo.com/ sasha13168

rocknrollforever: is that you or sabrina ?

lollybug3369: you know who it is. stop with the games.

rocknrollforever: lol

lollybug3369: we are friends now thanks to you

rocknrollforever: wow, you really have me at a lost here

rocknrollforever: i remember the pic

rocknrollforever: what the hell did i do ?!?!

lollybug3369: you know i dont like lol i never use it if you remember

lollybug3369: i only use lmao

rocknrollforever: tell me

lollybug3369: tell you what?

rocknrollforever: why are you so pissed at me ?

lollybug3369: what makes you think that i am pissed?

rocknrollforever: i dont know, just the way your talking to me

lollybug3369: i am not. just like messing with your head. like i said before.

lollybug3369: i am friends now with a few girls who you liked to play.

rocknrollforever: what ?

lollybug3369: bye sweetie

rocknrollforever: haha, now you have me confused

lollybug3369: it is ok that you are not that bright. I won't hold it against you.

rocknrollforever: haha, your talking in circles silly . . . hard to understand what your saying

rocknrollforever: first you tell me your from pa, then you tell me to look at your profile which says your from ny . . .

rocknrollforever: and you wont explain anything

rocknrollforever: so am i just suppose to guess ???

rocknrollforever: well ?

rocknrollforever: hello ???

rocknrollforever: ok, just ignore me then

rocknrollforever: well, you have a nice day now

lollybug3369:   you too, bye sweetie

A short while later, sasha began to chat with him. When he viewed sasha's profile, he noticed that lollybug's picture was on it. He got very angry and began to curse and swear. At that point in time, my computer guy yelled at me on the phone. He said to unplug the computer. Immediately I disconnected the power cord from the outlet.

"I am not sure how you figured out who this guy is. You are right. I know who this guy is."

"Then why did you have me disconnect my computer from the Internet?"

"He was sending code into our computers. This guy knows what he is doing. We need to keep one step ahead of him. Your intuition is unbelievable! How did you know he was in on it?"

"In one of my conversations with Mandel, he mentioned that I must have spoken with his cousin, Mike, the night before. It was not until later that this guy contacted me. I had used my Madonna identity. At the end of that conversation, I asked him what his name was. He said and I quote, 'Buttercup, mine is Mike.'

The chills ran up my spine. How could he have known that one of my identities was buttercup? I was logged on under my Madonna identity. Mike was supposedly Mandel's cousin's name. It was also the username of another person that was involved. It blew my mind that he knew the buttercup identity.

"Wow! Talking about blowing minds, you just blew mine. I cannot believe you figured out who this guy was. What are the odds?"

The information that these guys used on their profiles was made up. They never used their real names, locations, ages, and who knows, probably their sex. lol. Why would they? They were involved with stealing identities. I was on the quest to reveal their true identities. By exposing their faces with their usernames, real names, and phone numbers, this left them vulnerable, just like they tried to leave their victims.

Playing this trick on them left them confused and angry. Finally someone was better at their game then they were. This triggered violent reactions. Everything that they tried to do to retaliate backfired. Instead, they gave us evidence to prove who and where it was coming from. It was rather fun messing with their heads instead of them messing with mine. Revenge is the ultimate vindication.

Below is the chat of what Sasha said to rocknrollforever. He was too busy trying to figure out what lollybug's picture was doing on Sasha's profile. Then he tried executing a code to my computer guy's machine. What a mistake! This guy got very angry. It was as if it were a battle of who was the better hacker.

August 10, 2003

> *mrmagoo769* (8:44 PM):
>> sasha13168:   hi
>>
>> sasha13168:   how have you been
>>
>> sasha13168:   do you know your ass is mine, cause i know who you are now . . . . your world is getting smaller by the day
>
> *mrmagoo769* (9:09 PM) :
>> sasha13168:   you can't be serious, thats some pretty small time shit you are pullin over there
>
> *mrmagoo769* (9:10 PM) :
>> sasha13168:   my 8 year old can do better than that
>
> *mrmagoo769* (9:11 PM) :
>> sasha13168:   i took you down four years ago, that was nothing
>
> *mrmagoo769* (9:13 PM) :
>> sasha13168:   keep it up, you'll never get through this system, but thank you for all the evidence you have provided me with stupid

Chapter 5

Gathering of Evidence

For months, my computer served as the target of the hackers. My firewall documented all the hacking attempts. By continuing conversations with those whom I thought and suspected were involved in the hacking, I was able to gather additional information from those chats. In some cases, they gave me the names of computer programs that they were using. By researching the programs, I was able to determine whether they were working on a Mac or a PC.

By using reverse psychology, I was able to get them to volunteer information that I needed. When I received the names of the programs, I forwarded them to my computer guy. He in turn installed a program on my computer to combat the Yahoo! hackers.

While in chat with mikejoe, I mentioned to him that I was continuing my education in computers to fight the hackers. He asked me what I was learning. After telling him to watch his names list on Yahoo!, I proceeded to delete my username from his list right in front of his eyes.

He commented, "I am shocked that you are learning how to do this in school! I did not realize that they were allowed to teach these things." I had only told him that I was furthering my computer education and never said that I was going to school. Dealing with hackers meant that I had to think like they did.

Therefore, I was learning about the computer through online tutorials, special programs, and computer experts. By doing this, the hackers knew that I meant business. At least they knew I was relentless in my pursuit of justice.

"Fighting fire with fire is the only way for me to win this battle," I told him. Then I continued on, "Only the best teachers are instructing me. If I can understand how the hackers are doing these things to me and I have the knowledge to fight them back, perhaps I will scare them off and force them to leave me alone."

After removing my name from his list, he began to inquire how I did it. However, I would not tell him. Instead, I began to let him know how stupid the hackers really are. They were not even trying to hide their IP addresses from me. After telling them that their identities had all been exposed already and that I knew who they were and where they lived, a sense of justice was settling in. After all, they were not even trying to hide their IP addresses through proxy servers or even trying to bounce them.

The next day, all attempts to gain access into my computer were coming through proxy servers! They were already under surveillance and being watched. The police were already on to the fact that some crimes were being committed through other people's computers. After all, previous experience on my case taught them that.

By following each hacker's movements, they would be able to prove who was behind it. Although computers had been on the market for years, there were no laws on the books. New laws needed to be passed in order for these guys to be prosecuted.

Fortunately, one of the cases that evolved out of Operation Firewall was the one that involved the stolen identities of Senate committee members. Although I would never wish ill on anyone, it could not have happened to a better group of people. Now since they were personally affected by identity theft, they would cohesively work together in passing the laws needed to prosecute these hackers. This would speed up the justice system.

The following are a few chats in which we were tracking the hackers. We found quite a bit of comedy in between the lines, which kept us with a clear eye on what was happening. My persistence in tracking these guys made them very angry. Many attempts were made to access my computer to find out the current status of the investigation to no avail. There were many different people working on the investigation behind the scenes from many different agencies. My computer was the central target of these Internet criminals.

October 4, 2003

buttercup71190: look at the name that just hit me

buttercup71190: Time, Event, Intruder, Count
10/4/2003 12:04:20 PM, TCP_Probe_
MSRPC, SALVATION, 2

buttercup71190: lol

mrmagoo7:   too many coincidences, lol

mrmagoo7:   laptop still working too

mrmagoo7:   go figure

mrmagoo7:   now if i can resurrect killer, lol

buttercup71190: ok

mrmagoo7:   figure of speech, lol

mrmagoo7:   sorry

buttercup71190: np

buttercup71190: so what is ur backup plan?

mrmagoo7:   dunno yet

buttercup71190: im off phone now

mrmagoo7:   ok, give me a few please . . . .
tryin to rip killers guts out, lol

mrmagoo7:   so to speak

buttercup71190: ok

buttercup71190: np

mrmagoo7:   kool ending

buttercup71190: good

Yahoo! Messenger: mrmagoo7 has logged back in. (10/4/2003 10:19 PM)

buttercup71190: Time, Event, Intruder, Count

10/4/2003 10:38:39 PM, TCP_Probe_Sub7, nas1p50.clb.htcomp.net, 1

buttercup71190: Time, Event, Intruder, Count

10/4/2003 10:39:51 PM, TCP_Probe_Sub7, 6

mrmagoo7: six at once?

buttercup71190: yes

buttercup71190: only one minute apart from the previous time

mrmagoo7: popular tonight . . . . i got no hits at all

buttercup71190: 13 sub 7's some multiple times

mrmagoo7: damn, thats worse than usual

buttercup71190: yep

buttercup71190: must have been something i said

buttercup71190: lol

mrmagoo7: good thing they cant get in, lol

mrmagoo7: no wonder your machine was such a mess

buttercup71190: lol

mrmagoo7: oh man, easy kitty, hee hee

buttercup71190: lol

buttercup71190: told u they missed me

mrmagoo7: wait til they see you in a cape, lol

buttercup71190: or the leather catwoman suit

mrmagoo7:	well you should be in the leather catwoman suit and have a cape
mrmagoo7:	catwoman would look much classier in a cape
mrmagoo7:	sexy too
buttercup71190:	lol
buttercup71190:	look at the order of these probes within one minute of time
buttercup71190:	Time, Event, Intruder, Count

10/4/2003 10:38:39 PM, TCP_Probe_
Sub7, nas1p50.clb.htcomp.net, 1

Time, Event, Intruder, Count

10/4/2003 10:39:29 PM, TCP_Probe_
Other, USER1, 2

Time, Event, Intruder, Count

10/4/2003 10:39:51 PM, TCP_Probe_
Netbus, 3

Time, Event, Intruder, Count

10/4/2003 10:39:51 PM, TCP_Probe_
Sub7, 6

mrmagoo7:	damn, they want you bad
buttercup71190:	lol
buttercup71190:	did u see netbus and sub 7 at one time
buttercup71190:	9 attempts
mrmagoo7:	yes which means you should scan your machine tonight
buttercup71190:	that other probe was from DNS: rrcs-nyc-biz.rr.com
buttercup71190:	i think everything is coming through rr today
mrmagoo7:	still gettin hits?

buttercup71190: no

mrmagoo7:   want me to send ya some?, lol

buttercup71190: no ty that's ok

mrmagoo7:   i can send you a SBO

buttercup71190: lol

buttercup71190: go ahead and try

buttercup71190: u wont get in

mrmagoo7:   oh thems fightin talk lil lady, lol

buttercup71190: lol

buttercup71190: i think they missed me the past 4 days

mrmagoo7:   they aint missin ya now, lol

buttercup71190: they are missing my puter though

buttercup71190: lol

buttercup71190: boy rr is busy today

mrmagoo7:   get more hits?

buttercup71190: yes but not sub 7's

mrmagoo7:   good, when i get killer running, i'll test sub7 on your machine ok?

buttercup71190: you wouldn't

mrmagoo7:   hell no and face your wrath, lol

buttercup71190: then you would have to redo it again

buttercup71190: lol

October 19, 2003

Sweet Cheeks (9:24 PM) :

Time, Event, Intruder, Count

10/19/2003 9:18:49 PM, UDP_Probe_Trojan, cm.coyotecableconnections.com,5 mrmagoo769 (9:25 PM) :

> Time, Event, Intruder, Count
>
> 10/19/2003 8:44:36 PM, TCP_Probe_Sub7, hsdbrg.sasknet.sk.ca, 2

mrmagoo769 (9:25 PM) :

> damn, you got a problem

Sweet Cheeks (9:25 PM) :

> what?

mrmagoo769 (9:25 PM) :

> i think you better find someone to trust at your cable company

Sweet Cheeks (9:26 PM) :

> i know

mrmagoo769 (9:26 PM) :

> its either that or give up cable modem

Sweet Cheeks (9:26 PM) :

> lol

mrmagoo769 (9:26 PM) :

> give me a few days i have an idea

Sweet Cheeks (9:26 PM) :

> just might have to

Sweet Cheeks (9:26 PM) :

> K tell me

mrmagoo769 (9:26 PM) :

> not on here

mrmagoo769 (9:27 PM) :

> give me a while to work on it in my head

Sweet Cheeks (9:27 PM) :

> k

mrmagoo769 (9:27 PM) :

> you have some serious issues right now, i dont know who all is involved

October 26, 2003

mrmagoo769 (5:00 PM) :

hello, when did you sneak on here

Sweet Cheeks (5:00 PM) :

about 20 mins ago

Sweet Cheeks (5:01 PM) :

Time, Event, Intruder, Count

10/26/2003 4:41:46 PM, MSRPC_RemoteActivate_
Bo, .cm coyotecableconnections.com, 1

mrmagoo769 (5:01 PM) :

i had volume down, didnt see you

Sweet Cheeks (5:01 PM) :

i was on before you were on i thought

mrmagoo769 (5:01 PM) :

i know, i've been gettin slammed with
sub7's

mrmagoo769 (5:02 PM) :

no, i've been on for a while

Sweet Cheeks (5:02 PM) :

oh ok

mrmagoo769 (5:02 PM) :

icq has been acting up on me

Sweet Cheeks (5:02 PM) :

how so?

mrmagoo769 (5:03 PM) :

not showing people as on and it disconnects on
me

mrmagoo769 (5:03 PM) :

might be the server is full

Sweet Cheeks (5:03 PM) :

its doing the same thing to me

Sweet Cheeks (5:03 PM) :

> i get disconnected when i get those remote activate BO

mrmagoo769 (5:07 PM) :

> do you still have snagit on your puker?

Sweet Cheeks (5:08 PM) :

> not sure even if i did i dont have a printer lol

mrmagoo769 (5:08 PM) :

> well if you hadnt tried to print out your whole life on it, lol

Sweet Cheeks (5:08 PM) :

> lol

mrmagoo769 (5:09 PM) :

> i have a serial number for snagit virgin 6.11

Sweet Cheeks (5:09 PM) :

> add it to my cd

mrmagoo769 (5:10 PM) :

> yes dear

Sweet Cheeks (5:11 PM) :

> Time, Event, Intruder, Count
>
> 10/26/2003 5:10:24 PM, TCP_Probe_MSRPC. cm. coyotecableconnections.com, 1
>
> Time, Event, Intruder, Count
>
> 10/26/2003 5:10:43 PM, UDP_Probe_Other cm coyotecableconnections.com, 3
>
> they are getting ready to hit my puter again. lol

mrmagoo769 (5:11 PM) :

> this is not right ya know . . . .

Sweet Cheeks (5:11 PM) :

> i think 2 puters through my cable company are involved

Sweet Cheeks (5:12 PM) :

> this ip has hit me all day

Sweet Cheeks (5:12 PM) :

> then when they hit me with the remote activate BO it changes

mrmagoo769 (5:14 PM) :

> its possible they are doing it from the server itself

Sweet Cheeks (5:14 PM) :

> from there or elsewhere?

mrmagoo769 (5:14 PM) :

> yes

Sweet Cheeks (5:15 PM) :

> yes what?

mrmagoo769 (5:15 PM) :

> either or both

Sweet Cheeks (5:15 PM) :

> ohhhhhhhhhh

Sweet Cheeks (5:16 PM) :

> u think its the local stuff or nyc/nj

mrmagoo769 (5:17 PM) :

> i think you have both going on

Sweet Cheeks (5:17 PM) :

> iknow but the stuff from Coyote Cable Connections

mrmagoo769 (5:17 PM) :

> i cant be sure without going into your cable company's server

Sweet Cheeks (5:18 PM) :

> k

mrmagoo769 (5:32 PM) :

> icq is getting screwy

Sweet Cheeks (5:32 PM) :

it showed me the same thing about you

mrmagoo769 (5:35 PM) :

i'm doing some downloads, it may be interfering

Sweet Cheeks (5:44 PM) :

i think the guys are taking a dinner break

mrmagoo769 (5:44 PM) :

yes here too, lol . . . . shhhhhhhhhhhhhh

Sweet Cheeks (5:45 PM) :

maybe a new bomb in the artillery? lol

mrmagoo769 (5:45 PM) :

i hope so, i'm getting bored, lol

Sweet Cheeks (5:45 PM) :

lol i am getting sick of it

Sweet Cheeks (5:48 PM) :

i am getting nervous that they are changing
their attack plan.

Sweet Cheeks (5:49 PM) :

no phone, no access into house soon and no
puter access. what next?

mrmagoo769 (5:49 PM) :

dont matter if they do, they still cant get in

Sweet Cheeks (5:49 PM) :

not worried about the puter

mrmagoo769 (5:49 PM) :

gee maybe they will have to get a life!

Sweet Cheeks (5:49 PM) :

lol

Sweet Cheeks (5:50 PM) :

wont happen. they are sick

Sweet Cheeks (5:51 PM) :

have your friends emailed you or spoke with you?

mrmagoo769 (5:51 PM) :

nope havent heard a word yet

Sweet Cheeks (5:58 PM) :

adelphia is busy tonight

mrmagoo769 (5:58 PM) :

is that where its coming through?

Sweet Cheeks (5:59 PM) :

some of the probes are Y?

mrmagoo769 (5:59 PM) :

just wondering

Sweet Cheeks (6:00 PM) :

DNS: ny-lackawannacadent4-chtwga2b-c-187.
buf.adelphia.net

Sweet Cheeks (6:00 PM) :

DNS: oh-newphiladelphia2c-87.wre.adelphia.net

mrmagoo769 (6:01 PM) :

DNS: pcp03617246pcs.prtmry01.nj.comcast.net

Time, Event, Intruder, Count

10/26/2003 4:52:23 PM, TCP_Probe_Sub7,
pcp03617246pcs.prtmry01.nj.comcast.net, 1

Sweet Cheeks (6:02 PM) :

DNS: c-24-30-233-186.va.client2.attbi.com

Sweet Cheeks (6:02 PM) :

which is comcast

mrmagoo769 (6:50 PM) :

Time, Event, Intruder, Count

10/26/2003 6:49:43 PM, TCP_Probe_Sub7,
pcp01991468pcs.columb01.pa.comcast.net, 1

mrmagoo769 (6:50 PM) :

Time, Event, Intruder, Count

10/26/2003 6:53:30 PM, SQL_SSRP_StackBo,
bdsl._____.gte.net, 1

Sweet Cheeks (6:51 PM) :

lol

Sweet Cheeks (6:51 PM) :

Time, Event, Intruder, Count

10/26/2003 6:46:03 PM, TCP_Probe_MSRPC,_____.
cmcoyotecableconnections.com, 1

Time, Event, Intruder, Count

10/26/2003 6:47:19 PM, UDP_Probe_Other,
_____.cmcoyotecableconnections.com, 5

Time, Event, Intruder, Count

10/26/2003 6:48:22 PM, TCP_Probe_Other,
pool-_____.bos.east.verizon.net, 3

mrmagoo769 (6:51 PM) :

what no movie with their dinner?, lol

Sweet Cheeks (6:52 PM) :

those 2 probe from your cable company come
in simultaneously every time then they keep
doing the udp probe

Sweet Cheeks (6:53 PM) :

weird how i just got off the phone with you
and then i got hit immediately by verizon

mrmagoo769 (6:53 PM) :

yes i got it right away too

From August to December of 2003, I let my firewall program capture all the IP addresses involved in trying to enter my computer. Stack buffer overflows (SBO), Sub7, UDPs, Sun RPC, HTTP, MSRPC, FTP, NetBIOS, Netbus, LPR, Back Orifice, and other programs had no success.

Below is a sample of how easy it is to locate the information to hack user accounts right from the Internet. All you have to do is google the main keywords.

How to Hack Hotmail or Yahoo! Passwords

This is the best way to hack anyone's Hotmail or Yahoo! passwords. You can use your Hotmail address to get a Yahoo! address and vice versa also. Here is how to do it.

First, open a new e-mail message. Type in the To: box this e-mail address: pw_refresh_serv@hotmail.com. In the subject line, type "LOST PASSWORD." (Make sure to type this in uppercase as shown.) In the body, type on the first line your e-mail address (for example: you@hotmail.com or you@yahoo.com). On the third line, type your password. And on the fifth line, type the e-mail address of the person you are trying to get the password from (for example: them@hotmail.com or them@yahoo.com).

You must add <:/ text > so their server will read it as a command line.

Here is an example of what the e-mail should look like:

    TO: pw_refresh_serv@hotmail.com
    SUBJECT: LOST PASSWORD

    <:/ You@hotmail/yahoo.com.asi >

    <:/ 12345678.asi >

    <:/ Them@hotmail/yahoo.com.asi >

This is an administration privilege of the server via staff-member-formatted message (remember that Hotmail's server format is identically based on Yahoo!'s, so that is why you send it to Hotmail and not Yahoo!). *This information is for entertainment only and its authors do not advocate the stealing of passwords.*

Chapter 6

The Mousetrap

After collecting my firewall logs, for weeks, I decided to put the information into an Excel sheet. Numerous columns were created to store the information in a format that could be sorted in any way. The information included the date, time, type of probe, IP address, where the probe traveled through, and how many of packets of information were sent.

At the end of the night, I would usually sort the list by the IP address. Usually, one IP address would stand out. Patterns of attempted attacks would be evident when the excel sheet was sorted by time. Any time they sent a Sub 7, a stack buffer overflow would also be sent. Many times, the sub 7 would be sent in numerous packets, sometimes seven or nine at a time. Sorting the list by the server name would let me know where they were working through.

Now that my computer had been secured, it became a target computer of the hackers. They wanted to know what was going on. Since they were no longer in my computer, they could no longer see what we were up to. They only had to rely on our chats. After feeding them what I wanted them to think they knew, I could use other information to make them become fearful of me instead. Needing them to give me information, I had to withhold some things from them.

Sometimes I just used street smarts to gain information. That was how I gained the identity of one of the hackers. Playing the dumb blonde sometimes helped me. When they questioned me about programs that were on my computer, I must admit that I gave them the names of programs that were on my former computer or one that was not on my existing computer. Did they honestly think that I would tell them how my computer was secured? I'm not that naive.

Noticing that Mandel used an AOL account, I decided to open one for myself. Once AOL was downloaded to my computer, I taught myself the program. Then I decided to teach Mandel a final lesson.

After creating a new AOL account as catwoman900711, I began to message Mandel through his AOL account, nykaos or is that "New York Chaos"? I guess he felt obligated to live up to his name.

On Sunday, July 20, 2003, I had my final conversation with him.

catwoman900711 (5:22:39 PM):	meow
Nykaos4u (6:09:34 PM):	hello?
Nykaos4u (6:10:43 PM):	who r u
catwoman900711 (6:24:18 PM):	it's me catwoman
Nykaos4u (6:25:29 PM):	from where
catwoman900711 (6:25:48 PM):	Gotham city, or should I say
	Got 'em City. u?
Nykaos4u (6:25:53 PM):	funny
Nykaos4u (6:26:03 PM):	who r u and where did u get me screen name
catwoman900711 (6:26:12 PM):	u irish?
catwoman900711 (6:26:19 PM):	get me screen name?
catwoman900711 (6:26:22 PM):	lol
Nykaos4u (6:26:26 PM):	my

Nykaos4u (6:26:36 PM): what do u want

catwoman900711 (6:26:49 PM): to talk to you

Nykaos4u (6:26:53 PM): about

catwoman900711 (6:26:58 PM): ummmmmmmmmm

Nykaos4u (6:27:04 PM): where did u get my screen name

catwoman900711 (6:27:32 PM): through yahoo

Nykaos4u (6:27:36 PM): hmmm

Nykaos4u (6:27:44 PM): so who r u

catwoman900711 (6:27:45 PM): it was your email right?

Nykaos4u (6:28:05 PM): whats ur yahoo name

Nykaos4u (6:28:36 PM): ?

Nykaos4u (6:28:45 PM): hello

catwoman900711 (6:29:15 PM): you dont know who this is? i know who you are.

Nykaos4u (6:29:26 PM): hmmm

Nykaos4u (6:29:32 PM): whats your full screen name

catwoman900711 (6:29:56 PM): i just told you

Nykaos4u (6:30:11 PM): so where u from-i dont remember

catwoman900711 (6:30:31 PM): westchester

Nykaos4u (6:30:48 PM): u have a pic

catwoman900711 (6:31:04 PM): no i dont

catwoman900711 (6:31:07 PM): u?

Nykaos4u (6:31:17 PM): u tell me if u got my e-mail addy

Nykaos4u (6:31:22 PM): me

Nykaos4u (6:31:38 PM): whatcha wanna talk bout

catwoman900711 (6:31:53 PM): lol

catwoman900711 (6:32:11 PM):   is that a current pic?

Nykaos4u (6:32:50 PM):   maybe

Nykaos4u (6:32:58 PM):   tell me what u want

catwoman900711 (6:33:40 PM):   catwoman900711 (6:26:49 PM):   t o talk to you

Nykaos4u (6:33:47 PM):   about what

catwoman900711 (6:34:10 PM):   hmmmmmmmmmmm

catwoman900711 (6:34:23 PM):   ;-)

Nykaos4u (6:34:27 PM):   well . . .

Nykaos4u (6:34:56 PM):   i got no time for games so tell me

catwoman900711 (6:35:03 PM):   games?

catwoman900711 (6:35:26 PM):   that's what i heard you like to do

Nykaos4u (6:35:37 PM):   oh really-by whom

catwoman900711 (6:35:56 PM):   i know first hand

Nykaos4u (6:36:02 PM):   yea ok u know nothing

catwoman900711 (6:36:10 PM):   ok Bill Murray

Nykaos4u (6:36:23 PM):   oh wow scary u know my name

Nykaos4u (6:36:36 PM):   please girl what games r u talkij bout

Nykaos4u (6:36:40 PM):   talkin

catwoman900711 (6:36:45 PM):   it was not meant to be scary

Nykaos4u (6:37:01 PM):   well maybe one day i'll give u an autograph

catwoman900711 (6:37:07 PM):   lol

catwoman900711 (6:37:09 PM):   no thanks

Nykaos4u (6:37:09 PM):   so

Nykaos4u (6:37:19 PM):   what do u want to talk about

Nykaos4u (6:37:25 PM):   ?

catwoman900711 (6:37:38 PM): nothing

catwoman900711 (6:37:44 PM): i am done talking

Nykaos4u (6:37:48 PM):   oh

Nykaos4u (6:37:55 PM):   so whats the deal?

catwoman900711 (6:38:04 PM): deal?

Nykaos4u (6:38:06 PM):   yea

catwoman900711 (6:38:09 PM): no deal

Nykaos4u (6:38:27 PM):   so why arent u on yahoo?

catwoman900711 (6:38:46 PM): i have yahoo y?

Nykaos4u (6:38:55 PM):   so go onjline then

Nykaos4u (6:38:58 PM):   online

catwoman900711 (6:39:23 PM): no

Nykaos4u (6:39:26 PM):   y not

catwoman900711 (6:39:50 PM): i am on here

catwoman900711 (6:39:55 PM): isnt that enough?

Nykaos4u (6:40:00 PM):   u tell me

catwoman900711 (6:40:00 PM): brb

Nykaos4u (6:40:04 PM):   where u goin

catwoman900711 (6:43:23 PM): ib

Nykaos4u (6:43:29 PM):   ok

Nykaos4u (6:43:41 PM):   where did u go

catwoman900711 (6:44:04 PM): if you really must know to take a pisssssssssss

Nykaos4u (6:44:32 PM):   lol

Nykaos4u (6:44:46 PM):   so how far r u from nyc

catwoman900711 (6:45:15 PM): about 1/2 hour from queens

Nykaos4u (6:45:29 PM):   cool

Nykaos4u (6:46:04 PM):   so what nationality r u

catwoman900711 (6:46:16 PM): i am cat

catwoman900711 (6:46:21 PM): hear me purrrrrrrrrrrrr

Nykaos4u (6:46:30 PM): hmm ok i hope ur older then 12

catwoman900711 (6:46:38 PM): lol

Nykaos4u (6:46:52 PM): so what nationality r u

catwoman900711 (6:47:10 PM): american

catwoman900711 (6:47:13 PM): y?

catwoman900711 (6:47:23 PM): what are you?

Nykaos4u (6:47:28 PM): italian

Nykaos4u (6:48:37 PM): so whats up

Nykaos4u (6:49:06 PM): how many other screen names do u have?

catwoman900711 (6:49:14 PM): just a few y?

Nykaos4u (6:49:22 PM): what are they—the ones on yahoo

catwoman900711 (6:50:00 PM): u dont need to know. i am talking to you on here.

Nykaos4u (6:50:42 PM): so did u have a cam on yahoo?

catwoman900711 (6:50:53 PM): no

catwoman900711 (6:50:55 PM): u?

Nykaos4u (6:51:10 PM): nope

catwoman900711 (6:51:19 PM): then no use putting yahoo on.

Nykaos4u (6:51:28 PM): funny

Nykaos4u (6:51:33 PM): so what do u look like

catwoman900711 (6:51:50 PM): like catwoman

Nykaos4u (6:52:11 PM): hmmm human details please

catwoman900711 (6:52:19 PM): lol

catwoman900711 (6:52:37 PM): gorgeous curvacious body

Nykaos4u (6:53:00 PM): hmmmm

Nykaos4u (6:53:08 PM): u married

catwoman900711 (6:53:19 PM): of course not u?

Nykaos4u (6:53:40 PM): nope

Nykaos4u (6:53:42 PM): were u ever

catwoman900711 (6:53:50 PM): of course not u?

Nykaos4u (6:53:54 PM): nope

Nykaos4u (6:54:03 PM): so whats ur full screen name under yahoo

catwoman900711 (6:54:38 PM): you should know. we have spoken many times before.

Nykaos4u (6:54:46 PM): i dont remember honestly

Nykaos4u (6:55:04 PM): it must of been a long while

catwoman900711 (6:55:14 PM): not really

Nykaos4u (6:55:21 PM): when was the last time

catwoman900711 (6:55:30 PM): that we spoke on yahoo?

Nykaos4u (6:55:33 PM): yup

catwoman900711 (6:55:44 PM): about a week

Nykaos4u (6:55:56 PM): i doubt it-what did we talk about

catwoman900711 (6:56:13 PM): ;-)

Nykaos4u (6:56:23 PM): um tell me

catwoman900711 (6:56:55 PM): you honestly don't remember talking to me? :'(

Nykaos4u (6:57:07 PM): i dont for real-its been a rough week

catwoman900711 (6:57:17 PM): rough?

Nykaos4u (6:57:20 PM):   yea

catwoman900711 (6:57:36 PM): y?

Nykaos4u (6:57:39 PM):   just cause

Nykaos4u (6:57:49 PM):   so tell me what did we talk bout

Nykaos4u (6:58:13 PM):   ?

catwoman900711 (6:59:02 PM): you are such a con artist

catwoman900711 (6:59:11 PM): and liar

Nykaos4u (6:59:20 PM):   about what

Nykaos4u (6:59:32 PM):   ?

Nykaos4u (6:59:44 PM):   hello

Nykaos4u (6:59:56 PM):   do u know what a con artist is?

catwoman900711 (7:00:06 PM): yes you

Nykaos4u (7:00:24 PM):   ha funny-nooo im nopt sellinu something or tryin to trick u into anything

Nykaos4u (7:00:39 PM):   and what am i lyin about

catwoman900711 (7:01:06 PM): you tell me

Nykaos4u (7:01:21 PM):   no u tell me

Nykaos4u (7:02:22 PM):   u gonna tell me or what

catwoman900711 (7:02:32 PM): nope you know

Nykaos4u (7:02:38 PM):   i do huh

Nykaos4u (7:02:41 PM):   esplain please

Nykaos4u (7:03:30 PM):   ?

Nykaos4u (7:03:51 PM):   hello

catwoman900711 (7:04:19 PM): tired of talking and you not listening

Nykaos4u (7:04:32 PM):   ok

After messaging for about fifteen minutes, I finally told him something that he knew that I was the only one who knew. Then he realized who it was. Revenge was sweet. I could finally do to him what he had done to me.

"I didn't know that you had your computer repaired."

"Why would I let the hacker know my computer was repaired? My computer is new, and no one can get into it. I dare the hackers to try. At least now I can have some fun messing with their heads and lives. I don't get mad. I get even. I've had about all that I am going to take. Have a good life."

A sense of peace came over me. I now had control of my computer and my identity. It felt exhilarating to expose one of the hackers. I knew that my last conversation with him would tick him off. I needed for him to get angry with me. Now I knew that he would have to call in reinforcements. For the first time in months, I had gained control of my life. Determined that it was not going to happen to me again, I continued tracking the hackers.

It was ironic that I was able to log on with anonymity and the hackers had no idea that I was back online until I had messaged him. How dare a woman beat him at his own game! We were all on to him. By this point in time, I had my computer guy and his friends watching my computer. No one was going to be able to access my computer.

Chapter 7

Secret Society

*B*ehind the investigation were many people working toward the goal of arresting those who were perpetrating the crimes. In order to do this, they needed to enlist the help of another agency. While monitoring my computer, they were able to track the hacker's events. Sometimes it led them to other Web sites where the hacker was engaging in the purchase or the selling of people's personal identification. There were three major Web sites that were involved—Cruising-the-Shadows, CardingCrew, and DirtyMoney. These Web sites were selling people's names, addresses, credit card number, and expiration dates for a fee. In order to purchase such information, people needed to pay for the service with their credit card. Each Web site had over three thousand members who were trafficking in these illegal activities. That was one issue.

The secret society of hackers was behind this. Not only were the hackers interested in stealing peoples' identities, they also found another way to spy on them. This meant that the hackers had remote control of a person's webcam. This was what the government referred to as access-device fraud. People's webcams were being activated without their knowledge or permission. The video was being uploaded to Web sites where people would pay to view.

In the course of several weeks, thousands of webcams were being activated without people's consent. The secret society of ethical hackers devised a program that would allow the victim to be warned that they were being watched. A pop-up would appear across their desktop. It was a picture of a skull with crossbones along with the message "We are watching you." What would be the first logical reaction to seeing such a pop-up? The first thing that I would do is unplug the computer. When people started unplugging their computers, the hackers had no video to upload. This would hurt their business.

The very first thing that occurred upon the activation of the pop-up program was that code was executed to the victim's computer to retrieve personal e-mail addresses. This information was gathered by the secret society that was in charge of gathering this information. Once the hackers realized something was going on, they were bent on finding out who was behind this. After all, they were losing money.

Several weeks after the inception of this pop-up program, an e-mail blast was sent out to all the victims. They were told to contact the local FBI office. The FBI only gets involved if a crime occurs over state lines. In this case, many state lines were being crossed. In a short period of time, the FBI received over two thousand complaints. Now the FBI could start their investigation into this access-device fraud.

Computers had been out for many years. However, there were no laws on the books for any computer crimes. After the Secret Service, Department of Justice, and FBI saw the crimes being committed, new legislation was put on the agenda. In order to arrest anyone involved in any computer crime, there needed to be laws. How could the government have allowed people to commit crimes over the Internet for many years and still have no laws on the books? Now there was a rush to get the laws passed. Crimes such as identity theft, drug trafficking, fraudulent wire transfers, and kidnappings were all being done with the aid of the Internet. There were Web sites where anyone could find out how to do any of these things. Explicit instructions were given on the Internet detailing how to commit these crimes even for someone who had no background or knowledge in computers. How could our own government allow such information for the public to view without considering the ramifications of the potential fraud?

The Internet had never been policed before this case. Yet over the years, millions of dollars, perhaps billions of dollars were being paid out by insurance companies and credit card companies for the fraud. Operation Firewall had started over four thousand investigations. Many different agencies were involved in different aspects of the case. The United States Security and Exchange Commission got involved when the File was found on the hacker's server. Other agencies such as FISA and NASA were involved in tracking many of the hackers, the File, and me.

Initially, I was told that I was in the witness protection plan, the watchful eye version. This would mean that I could remain where I was without having to be relocated. Many agents were assigned to watch me and the events that were going on around me. Not once did the government advise me of what my legal rights were. The case had been classified. Knowing that meant I was not able to discuss the case with anyone except my computer guy and my mother. Not once did I ever see a contract or agreement from them that discussed any of the details. It was Operation Firewall that led to the admission that the government was in the business of the domestic spy program. Most of the spying was being done without warrants and with warrantless wiretapping. By not entering into any written or oral contract with me, this has been a protection for me. Being under no obligations to anyone in my case, it has given me the freedom to speak about the case now. To this day, I still don't understand how the president gave himself these expanded powers and got away with it. The real thoughts and intentions of George Bush toward me will later be revealed.

Approximately one year had passed since I had discovered my computer was hacked. However, my Internet service provider still had not done anything to stop the attempts to hack my computer. In fact, they allowed their own server to act as the catalyst to perpetrate the crimes. My frustration with their lack of interest and concern led me to go to the top management and seek justice.

Below is the copy of the original letter I sent them documenting my ordeal. Their lack of action made my blood boil. This led me to go to the top of their chain.

March 20, 2004

Coyote Cable Connections
xxxxx
xxxxxxxx, xx xxxxx

ATT: Stuart Reynolds
Operations Manager

Stuart:

As per my phone conversation with Don, yourself, and James, my computer guy, on Friday, March 19th, 2004, I am following up with a letter detailing my problems with my computer security and why I feel that some of your employees might be involved.

Let me start by saying, thank you for looking into this matter. It means a lot to me that someone is finally taking me serious.

I had a long conversation with Rhonda yesterday. You forwarded me some notes. I want it on record that these notes were altered and not the original notes that she typed. Names were omitted as well as some of the main information. At least it provides me with an outline to go by since so much has happened in the past year.

In February of 2003, I switched over from telephone access to a one-way cable modem. That seems to be when my problems started. Your tech department was notified of all of the internet access problems I was having. On one occasion, Craig came to my house and told me the problem was the firewall. So he disabled it. I reactivated it after he left. I had been able to get online for days before that. Therefore, I knew it could not be the firewall. The problem was usually on Coyote Cable Connections' end. They had to release and renew the IP address numerous times and usually that cleared up the problem. Since the one way cable modem service was new, I expected there to be some bugs.

On one occasion, Craig and Bill came to my house to fix my modem problems. Supposedly, Bill works at your company. He is middle aged, gray hair, missing some teeth. It was not until November that Bill signed up on my new internet store that got me thinking. I called you to see if he was in. No one knew him or so I was told. So who was the guy in my home when Craig was here? However, there is someone there by the name of Bill something. I think it was McGuiness.

In April of 2003, I had discovered that my computer had been hacked. I had received a message from someone telling me that they were stalking me. At this point in time, I contacted the NYS Police, Internet Crime Division out of Middletown, NY, an officer by the name of Investigator Paul. At this time, I also contacted Craig at your company. I explained that I was receiving threatening e-mails all of which I had saved after the viruses were quarantined. He told me to forward them to him and that he would trace them. Later, he told me that they could not be traced. At this point in time, I told him that I had someone stalking me through Yahoo! and asked if he knew anything about tracing who he or she was. He told me that he did not know but that he knew someone that could help me. I gave him my information for his friend to contact me.

About a week later, a guy contacted me saying that Craig told him about my dilemma. He offered to help. After a few lengthy conversations on the computer, I contacted him by telephone. He offered to come up to my house and download a few programs to protect my computer and scan my computer. I had my neighbor come over to the house for the day so that there would be two of us to witness what he did. While there, this guy, Brian Sugarloaf bragged to my friend and me that his claim to fame was how many Yahoo! accounts he has hijacked. In fact, he showed us both how to do it and actually hijacked someone's account right from my computer! I believe this is how he keeps from being caught. If that account was ever researched, it would be my IP that shows up that hijacked the account. I believe the hackers use other people's computers and I know for a fact that they use other people's Yahoo!, AOL, etc. and e-mail accounts. I thanked him for what he did to supposedly secure my computer and he left.

The next day online, he contacted me by instant message. I thanked him again. The first part of the conversation was okay but then he started to get vulgar and profane with me. So before I chose to ignore him, I logged into my current yahoo account that I was using and changed my password. Then I blew him off and told him I did not want to ever talk to him again. I then tried to log into my other Yahoo! account but it had already been hijacked.

The next day I contacted the NYS Police Internet Crime Division and told Investigator Paul about what had happened. At that time, Brian tried to talk to me again somehow removing his name off of my ignore list. So I placed it back on ignore. Then he tried to boot me offline. He could not do that since I had downloaded a program to prevent me from getting booted. I was in chat with the NYS Police when he did this. However, since he could not boot me, he did in fact boot the officer. Not only did he boot him, but he also hijacked his account right in front of him!

I then contacted Craig. I asked him if he knew Brian. He said no. Yet I told him that Brian Sugarloaf contacted me using his name. He said he did not know anyone by that name.

Now, I contacted James, my computer guy, out of Florida to inquire about what might be wrong in my internet security. I told him what had just happened. I mentioned that I thought I knew who had hijacked my account, someone by the name of Brian. He then said that he knew him. Both Brian and Craig worked at Coyote Cable Connections together and met James at his computer store.

I outlined all of my problems I was having with my computer and he suggested that I wipe my hard drive and reinstall everything new. Therefore, he had my hard drive wiped only after saving it to ghost copy. Everything was reinstalled new from CD so as not to re-infect my computer with anything. A firewall and anti-virus program were installed prior to going online. At this time, I called Coyote Cable Connections, my cable company, to change my IP address. I was told that only Craig and Steve were able to do this. Craig was in. So I had no choice but to change it through him. While changing my IP address, he suggested I change the password on my e-mail account too knowing all of the problems I was having. Then my computer was put online. So now, it was as if I was a totally new customer online and no one previously could find me. However, within 10 minutes I was hit with one Trojan and two key loggers. The only IP that was allowed to bypass my firewall was my cable company since I use them for internet access.

Then I started to receive numerous attempts to place Trojans and key loggers into my computer. I received 100's of each of Sub 7's, stack buffer overflows, back orifice, remote activate buffer overflows (all of which were from your IP's), and other program attempts. At this point in time, I contacted the tech department letting them know that all of these remotes were coming through them and that I wanted it to stop. At that time, I dealt with Steve who did nothing for my problems. I then went over his head to Don. At this point in time, I told him what I had suspected. The remotes then seemed to have stopped.

Shortly after during this past fall, Coyote Cable Connections came to my house to install a two-way modem. However, a few days later, I had problems getting online. So they scheduled someone to come up to the house. Some guy showed up in November or December and started rummaging through my computer looking at what software programs and security programs that I had on here. Once again, the problem was on your end not mine. Not once that whole year was the problem ever on my end.

Then I had people calling me up telling me that they sent me e-mail of which I had never replied. I told them that I never got it. In fact, while all of this was going on, I only had two rentals that summer. The only business e-mail that I got was from websites that actually e-mail me with inquiries. I never received one e-mail from my website directly. I contacted your tech department. I explained my problem with my business e-mail. Once again, Craig had answered the phone. He told me to check my e-mail server address. He told me to change it to mail.coyotecableconnections. com. Then all of the sudden I dropped down to less than nine e-mails a day. Once again, I called the tech department. Craig answered again. I told him that I went from getting 70 plus e-mails a day down to nine a day. He told me that a new filter was placed on the e-mail server. I told him that I did not want my e-mail filtered. He said that it would not affect my business e-mail but would only delete the spam mail that had unrecognizable words. A few days later, I called back. This time someone else answered. I told him what was going on. He had me check the server addresses. He said to change it to incoming. coyotecableconnections. com and outgoing. coyotecableconnections.com. He said that there have been numerous problems with that server and that they do NOT use that one anymore. He told me that it was possible that my e-mail was being deleted or that virus problems would occur more with the e-mail. After making this change two weeks ago, it seems that I am once again receiving sixty plus e-mails a day. In fact, I received my first business e-mail right through my site last night after my call to you earlier that day for the first time in almost a year. In addition, when logging on for my e-mail I would receive numerous Trojan attempts such as win crash, bo bo, psyber streaming, etc. With the security on my computer, nothing can get installed without me seeing it first. The only way that could happen would be if someone actually installed the Trojan right on my computer when they were working on it.

Without your knowledge, all of my business e-mail for my website was going to my computer guy as well as my regular e-mail account for the past month or so. Yet James was receiving three times the amount of e-mail than I was. This past winter, I did not receive one e-mail from my website. I only received e-mails from other sites that notify me of any inquiries. This is a problem since the wintertime is my busy season for rentals. The summer is the second busiest season during which I had problems receiving my e-mails too. In fact, during the summer, the NYS Police, Internet

Crime Division sent me e-mails through my website of which I never received. This e-mail tampering has cost me a lot of loss of rentals and income. This does not even include the added expense that I had to incur due to the hacking including the computer security, not to mention the emotional stress placed upon me by loss of income, loss of privacy and identity theft. These people have not only hacked into my computer but they hacked into my life and I need it to stop!

The phone call to you was prompted by a reaction I got from your tech department earlier that morning. I spoke with someone and informed them that I had received a mime compliant e-mail client attachment buffer overflow right from the cable company's server the night before at 3/18/2004 8:31:27 PM, POP_Filename_Overflow, headend. coyotecableconnections.com, 2 attempts, IP address xxxxxx which is your mail server! This IP I tried to block that night. However, when I logged on the next day, I could not download my e-mail not realizing this IP was your mail server and that I had blocked it. I spoke with someone in your tech department who told me to telnet coyotecableconnections. I could only telnet coyotecableconnectionsonline.net and not coyotecableconnections.com. Yet I was able to surf the internet. Then it dawned on me that I blocked one of your IP's the night before. Therefore, I unblocked it. Then it worked. I told the guy what had happened the night before. I told him that I had some problems with some people who were trying to hack my computer. I told him that many of my problems were coming through your servers. He laughed at me. That just infuriated me to the point of no return.

That same day, March 19, 2004 when your tech guy laughed at me, just before I called you, the straw that broke the camel's back was when I gave the IP address to James to trace for me. Someone executed code to his computer causing a memory dump. Fortunately, he can retrieve the information since he does backups of his hard drive. These are the same memory dumps that had been done on my computer in an attempt to try to erase any traces of what they were doing and where it was coming from. Luckily, copies of the information including firewall logs, log files of all types and text files were kept in duplicate, triplicate, or even more and done in more than one location. Therefore, there is no loss of information.

For months, I had been calling different ones at your company and explaining my concerns and yet NOT ONE PERSON there took me seriously. It was then that I decided to call the owner and President of your company, James. It was not until I spoke with Rhonda and outlined my problems to her, that I finally got a response of concern. That was only after I put my foot down and demanded satisfaction or else I would seek resolution to my problems through any other agency that could help me including Internic.

Not only do I believe that my e-mail was being tampered with, I believe they were trying to gain access to my computer through the e-mail account. In fact, I also believe that my IP address is being monitored by them. After logging on, I usually receive a stack buffer over flow or sub seven attempts. Then after I download my e-mail, I received a Trojan of some type trying to access my computer. Therefore, even if they cannot get in my computer, they know when I am online. I have changed my IP so many times and it does not matter. They know when I am on.

I hope that I have reached a hearing ear. I look forward to resolving this matter as soon as possible. As I said earlier, this e-mail tampering has cost me a lot including loss of rentals and income. This does not even include the added expense that I had to incur due to the hacking including the computer security, not to mention the emotional stress placed upon me by loss of income, loss of privacy and identity theft. These people have not only hacked into my computer but they hacked into my life and I need it to stop! Please do what you can to stop this. I am hoping that you keep in touch with my computer guy as he can supply you with information that is more specific.

I look forward to putting this matter behind me soon. Copies on disc of my security log files are available to you upon request.

Thank you,

Angela Hart

As a side note, they never did ask for my security log files. Prior to writing this book, I had asked them for their explanation as to the events surrounding the investigation. However, their response was not truthful, so I decided to publish the truth myself. Always giving people the benefit of the doubt, I was hoping for a response that I could use. Unfortunately, the man to whom I addressed this letter has passed away. Many of the people referred to in this letter still work for them, although names have been changed or omitted.

Chapter 8

Operation Firewall

mrmagoo7:   my friends tested the security on your machine a few weeks ago, and were very impressed

mrmagoo7:   they cant unfortunately get into ur puter

hack::vindicator4u: say hi for me to your friends

mrmagoo7:   nobody is in the room yet

hack::vindicator4u: by what you secured my puter with?

mrmagoo7:   yes

hack::vindicator4u: they couldn't get in?

hack::vindicator4u: lol

mrmagoo7:   nope

mrmagoo7:   they tried for about an hour, lol

hack::vindicator4u: no way

mrmagoo7:   because i hadnt put any new updates in there for a while they thought they could break thru, lol

mrmagoo7:   dumbasses

mrmagoo7:	they werent gonna go in, just wanted to see if they could is all
hack::vindicator4u:	did they have fun trying at least? lol
mrmagoo7:	friggin pukers anyway
mrmagoo7:	now i have to log back into the room again, brb
hack::vindicator4u:	k
hack::vindicator4u:	did u want the cam off?
mrmagoo7:	yes you can turn it off now
mrmagoo7:	was testing the connection
mrmagoo7:	ty
mrmagoo7:	bbiab
hack::vindicator4u:	k
mrmagoo7:	ib finally
hack::vindicator4u:	wb finally lol
mrmagoo7:	so, how was your day?
hack::vindicator4u:	good
hack::vindicator4u:	so what is new tonight?
mrmagoo7:	they are just doing updates at the moment, blah blah blah
hack::vindicator4u:	what updates?
mrmagoo7:	just bringing everyone up to date on policies and stuff
hack::vindicator4u:	k
mrmagoo7:	should i give em the bad news tonight or wait, lol
hack::vindicator4u:	bad news?
mrmagoo7:	yeah i'm gonna leave the group
hack::vindicator4u:	all because they wont tell u about the alamo? lol
mrmagoo7:	no, lol
hack::vindicator4u:	jc

hack::vindicator4u: lol

mrmagoo7: no because i'm not gonna do anymore work for them

hack::vindicator4u: k

mrmagoo7: i'm letting em know tonight that i'm not doing anymore work for free at all period

hack::vindicator4u: i dont blame u

mrmagoo7: i dont mind doing the room and code that pertains to the group stuff

hack::vindicator4u: tell them that

hack::vindicator4u: but u cant spend hours working for them for free

mrmagoo7: i am, i will however do it for 800.00 per session

hack::vindicator4u: lol

hack::vindicator4u: ok

mrmagoo7: no that the rate

hack::vindicator4u: i know

mrmagoo7: thats what everyone else is charging right now for a 10 minute session

hack::vindicator4u: wow

mrmagoo7: my last job should have paid 1800.00 for 22 minutes

mrmagoo7: and i did submit them a bill for it

hack::vindicator4u: maybe u should explain to them that u have fell so far behind because of having to do all of this work and cant do it for free anymore

hack::vindicator4u: or i can tell them lol

mrmagoo7: well i posted the bill to see how they react to it

hack::vindicator4u: and?

mrmagoo7:   they havent seen it yet

hack::vindicator4u: k

mrmagoo7:   about 5 minutes they will get to it

hack::vindicator4u: k

hack::vindicator4u: did they see ur other message? lol

mrmagoo7:   gonna be an interesting meeting

mrmagoo7:   oh yes, that came up

hack::vindicator4u: and? can i tell u yet?

mrmagoo7:   absolutely, lol

hack::vindicator4u: lol

mrmagoo7:   is your machine getting hit right now?

mrmagoo7:   ftp

hack::vindicator4u: no

mrmagoo7:   k, jc

hack::vindicator4u: y?

hack::vindicator4u: u hitting me?

mrmagoo7:   how bout now?

hack::vindicator4u: nothing

mrmagoo7:   k

hack::vindicator4u: am i supposed to?

mrmagoo7:   no you shouldnt see anything

hack::vindicator4u: cool

mrmagoo7:   i just hit your machine with a few things

mrmagoo7:   nothing got thru

hack::vindicator4u: and y are we doing this?

mrmagoo7:   testing a new protocol from the group

mrmagoo7:   bunch of dummies

hack::vindicator4u: lol

hack::vindicator4u: this firewall takes a while to log the hits

hack::vindicator4u: i did get them

mrmagoo7: ty

mrmagoo7: what do the logs show?

hack::vindicator4u: some high rated hits it does not read like black ice used to

mrmagoo7: k

mrmagoo7: well it doesnt really matter as long as the software you have keeps the computer secure

hack::vindicator4u: k

hack::vindicator4u: but black ice was really good to me and i miss it

hack::vindicator4u: lol

mrmagoo7: well once i get the router on there you wont see anything any more

hack::vindicator4u: and that will be in another year or so? lol

mrmagoo7: it better not or i'll call that damn bank myself, lol

hack::vindicator4u: lol

mrmagoo7: ok, they are trying to get all of the arrest records and court information for all of the cases

hack::vindicator4u: for what purpose?

mrmagoo7: for us

hack::vindicator4u: u mean we will find out who they all are?

mrmagoo7: they cannot just request certain ones, they have to request all of them

mrmagoo7: yes if they get the files they are requesting

hack::vindicator4u: oh shit

hack::vindicator4u: that's a lot

mrmagoo7: yeah you dont wanna know, lol

hack::vindicator4u: how many now?

mrmagoo7: upwards around 56,000 people so far in connection with all of these cases

hack::vindicator4u: no way!!!

mrmagoo7: yes way . . . .

hack::vindicator4u: y do i have such a hard time comprehending this?

mrmagoo7: they have confiscated dig this; over 19,000 personal computers and over 1,000 servers

hack::vindicator4u: wow

mrmagoo7: the evidence is taking up 2 warehouses

hack::vindicator4u: wow

hack::vindicator4u: under guard i am sure lol

mrmagoo7: well naturally

mrmagoo7: federal property

hack::vindicator4u: y does this not feel real to me?

hack::vindicator4u: any "Design-a-Site" arrests yet? lol

mrmagoo7: probably because of the magnitude of the whole thing

mrmagoo7: and no on "Design-a-Site"

hack::vindicator4u: that will come soon lol

hack::vindicator4u: they are totally revamping the internet with all of this

mrmagoo7: they are changing everything over this

mrmagoo7: with all of the law changes, internet security changes, spam laws, sites being taken down . . . .

mrmagoo7:   it shouldnt be too hard to comprehend that this thing is so big

hack::vindicator4u: lots of sites

mrmagoo7:   thousands of web sites are now totally gone

hack::vindicator4u: it needed to be cleaned out

mrmagoo7:   alot more are being shut down as we speak

mrmagoo7:   wb

hack::vindicator4u: what happened? u boot me? lol

mrmagoo7:   no i dont think so, lol

mrmagoo7:   want me to?, lol

hack::vindicator4u: no ty

mrmagoo7:   k, jc honey

hack::vindicator4u: do ur friends know who is who in the arrests? or they will when they get the info?

mrmagoo7:   no they wont know until they get all the files

mrmagoo7:   and sort em, lol

hack::vindicator4u: how many files is that? lol

mrmagoo7:   and i aint doin it, lol

hack::vindicator4u: i'll help lol

hack::vindicator4u: i want to know

hack::vindicator4u: now!!!!!!!!!!!!!!

mrmagoo7:   you do that, lol

hack::vindicator4u: ok

mrmagoo7:   i told em

hack::vindicator4u: lol

mrmagoo7:   ok, but you have to go to dc

hack::vindicator4u: let me know when, i'll take some time off work

hack::vindicator4u: lol

mrmagoo7: lol

hack::vindicator4u: i have waited a few years for this lol

hack::vindicator4u: tell them i'll do a spreadsheet for them with everyone listed lol

mrmagoo7: oh yeah good luck, that will only take about a month

hack::vindicator4u: i know sa

hack::vindicator4u: lol

Behind the investigation were many people working toward the goal of arresting those who were perpetrating the crimes. In order to do this, they needed to enlist the help of another agency. While monitoring my computer, they were able to track the hacker's events. Sometimes it led them to other Web sites where the hacker was engaging in the purchase or the selling of people's personal identification. There were three major Web sites that were involved—Cruising-the-Shadows, CardingCrew, and DirtyMoney. These Web sites were selling people's names, addresses, credit card number, and expiration dates for a fee. In order to purchase such information, people needed to pay for the service with their credit card. Each Web site had over three thousand members who were trafficking in these illegal activities.

Two of these Web sites resulted in the arrest of over three thousand members, and the third Web site resulted in the arrest of over four thousand members. The shutting down of these three Web sites that were trafficking in stolen credit card information and identities now brought the total arrests to over ten thousand people. This was treated as a separate investigation.

Watching the hackers' movements would lead the authorities to many more arrests. In fact, there were several big identity thefts that were in the news as a result. There was the arrest of the man who had stolen 140,000,000 identities through AOL. There were the arrests of numerous people involved with the MasterCard/Visa identity thefts. Paris Hilton's address book was stolen through T-Mobile by one of the original hackers that had stolen my identity. There was the DSW, the Sports Authority, T.J. Maxx, Marshalls, and many other retail merchants who were also victims of these hackers.

Many new departments were formed within the government, such as ICE. This agency was responsible for enforcing a broad range of laws related to financial crime, customs and export violations, and other cross-border crimes. The agency's professional investigators played a vital role in countering the tactics that criminal and terrorist organizations employ to circumvent the law, whether it is fighting money laundering, bulk cash smuggling, intellectual property violations, weapons trafficking, drug smuggling, or any of the Murrieta customs crimes under their authority.

The long-awaited phone call finally came. It was on October 28, 2004. After spending a beautiful day attending my friend's wedding on the boat on Lake George, upon returning home, I got good news! It was about a year and a half after the investigation started before the first arrests were finally made. There were twenty-eight people in the United States and twenty overseas that were arrested. This was music to my ears. When I received the phone call that the first arrests had been made, I was elated.

Chapter 9

The Arrests

*L*isten **(AP)** Federal authorities on Thursday charged 19 people in the United States and abroad with operating a Web site that investigators claimed was one of the largest online centers for trafficking in stolen identity information and credit cards.

The site, www.Cruising-the-Shadows.com, had about 4,000 members who dealt with at least 1.7 million stolen credit card numbers and caused more than $4 million in losses, the U.S. Department of Justice said.

A 62-count indictment handed up by a federal grand jury in Newark said the site was dedicated to aiding computer hackers and also distributed stolen bank account numbers and counterfeit documents, such as drivers' licenses, passports and Social Security cards.

The investigation has led to the arrest of 21 people in the United States, and about 20 overseas. Some have not yet been indicted, authorities said.

It followed a yearlong undercover investigation by the Secret Service and other agencies, the Justice Department said.

The Cruising-the-Shadows' site on Thursday declared it is "For those who wish to play in the shadows!"

It listed several discussion groups including one on "novelty identification, 2nd ID, Passports, and the like." Another focused on "hacking, SPAM, online anonymity tools and programs in general."

A contact person for the Web site was not immediately found.

The indictment includes charges of conspiracy, trafficking in stolen credit card numbers and unlawful transfer of identification documents, among others. The penalties range from three years to 15 years in prison. The list of those arrested can be found online by searching "Firewall Indictment".

buttercup71190:	i went to Cruising-the-Shadows' site, now i hope i don't get investigated LOL
mrmagoo7:	what are you up to?
buttercup71190:	my mom said she found an article stating that some were arrested for sexual crimes
buttercup71190:	reading your email
mrmagoo7:	cool, have her send me that article please
mrmagoo7:	k
buttercup71190:	she's dropping it off to me later after she cleans
mrmagoo7:	cool, scan it for me

buttercup71190: k

buttercup71190: i hope it has the web address

buttercup71190: then u only need the link

mrmagoo7:   yup

buttercup71190: she typed in hackers

buttercup71190: and got into a wrong site LOL

mrmagoo7:   be careful doing that, most hack sites grab your machine when you enter their site

buttercup71190: i know

buttercup71190: i told her

buttercup71190: she didnt listen lol

mrmagoo7:   oh like you right?, lol

buttercup71190: ha ha ha

buttercup71190: i went to Cruising-the-Shadows' site, now i hope i dont get investigated lol

mrmagoo7:   oh now your screwed, lol

buttercup71190: yea yea

buttercup71190: lol

mrmagoo7:   watch for black sedans parked outside

buttercup71190: The charges against individual suspects range from conspiring to commit identity fraud, exchanging 18 million e-mail accounts along with personal identifying information, trafficking in credit card numbers, and exchanging forged and stolen identification documents

mrmagoo7:   yes thats what i read

buttercup71190: "We'll continue our investigation and we have, pursuant to court order, seized quite a bit of information. We'll

	be looking at that and we'll continue to pursue people who steal other people's information," he said.
buttercup71190:	http://www.internetnews.com/security/article.php/3429101
mrmagoo7:	reading
mrmagoo7:	interesting
buttercup71190:	yea
buttercup71190:	Operation Firewall began in July 2003 as an investigation in access device fraud before expanding into an investigation of global credit card fraud and identity theft fraud.
mrmagoo7:	i checked all the local jersey papers, didnt find much
buttercup71190:	http://www.securityfocus.com/news/9831
mrmagoo7:	you have mail
buttercup71190:	k
buttercup71190:	Among those arrested was a 19 year-old from Camberley, Surrey, who was picked up on Wednesday (27 October).
buttercup71190:	http://www.theregister.co.uk/2004/10/29/operation_firewall/
mrmagoo7:	http://www.secretservice.gov/
mrmagoo7:	quit foolin around, lol
buttercup71190:	booted
mrmagoo7:	see you shouldnt have gone to that site!
buttercup71190:	lol
mrmagoo7:	In August, the FBI seized computers in five states as part of Operation Digital Gridlock, the first federal action against criminal copyright piracy of

movies, games, software, and music over peer-to-peer networks.

Also in August, the FBI's Operation Web Snare snapped up more than 150 suspects in a variety of cybercrimes, including spamming, identity theft, and hacking.

mrmagoo7: http://news.zdnet.
co.uk/0,39020330,39171958,00.htm

mrmagoo7: Beginning in early 2004, data obtained through court authorized intercepts revealed internal communications, transactions and practices of the previously identified groups and other criminal organizations. The amount of information gathered during the investigation is approximately two terabytes—the equivalent of an entire university's academic library."

mrmagoo7: http://news.zdnet.co.uk/internet/ security/0,39020375,39171937,00.htm

mrmagoo7: ok knock it off, lol

buttercup71190: lol

mrmagoo7: A grand jury indictment delivered on Thursday in New Jersey found that 19 members of an online site, Cruising-the-Shadows.com, traded tutorials and information about identity theft and forgery and exchanged sensitive personal and financial information. The charges against individual suspects range from conspiring to commit identity fraud, exchanging 18 million email accounts along with personal identifying information, trafficking in credit card numbers, and exchanging forged and stolen identification documents.

buttercup71190: Andrew and Brandon were arrested in connection with the operation of www.Cruising-the-Shadows.com, a Web site that investigators say served as an online bazaar for counterfeit documents.

buttercup71190: save these names

buttercup71190: http://www.azcentral.com/community/ scottsdale/articles/1030sr-idtheft30Z8. html

mrmagoo7: yeah those guys are in arizona i think

mrmagoo7: i have info on them from their machines

buttercup71190: good

mrmagoo7: its all been turned in months ago

mrmagoo7: i am wiping killer clean after i make sure they have everything else i have

mrmagoo7: i think i've done my part to get even with all the hackers who have hurt me or my friends, time to hang up my cape, lol

buttercup71190: lol

buttercup71190: so who did u turn the info in to?

mrmagoo7: i think it ended up at the justice department eventually

mrmagoo7: i turned it in to the group

buttercup71190: ok

buttercup71190: so they know how this whole investigation started?

mrmagoo7: all of your log files were turned in as well

buttercup71190: oh wow lol

mrmagoo7: everything i got off your old machine, your chats-it all went

buttercup71190: lol

buttercup71190: u were busy

mrmagoo7: yes i figure i spent a total of about a thousand hours on it

buttercup71190: wow

mrmagoo7: i even retrieved some of lauries info and sent that along too

buttercup71190: how did that help?

mrmagoo7: similar chats key phrases and such, also the programs they used to compromise her machine and her log files

buttercup71190: how did the chats help?

mrmagoo7: what is going on tonight over there?

buttercup71190: some of the sites i am going to are booting me

buttercup71190: keep getting back end connections through yahoo

mrmagoo7: oh ok

buttercup71190: But it could have been worse. Estimates of potential damages if the gangs hadn't been broken up range into the hundreds of millions, the agency said.

buttercup71190: too bad we cant get a percentage of what we saved people as well as a reward LOL

mrmagoo7: rewards may be pending

buttercup71190: really?

mrmagoo7: but dont count on it for at least a year

mrmagoo7: yes really

buttercup71190: i didnt think they would do that

mrmagoo7: oh yeah by the time they finish this it will total into at least 20 million worth of damages

buttercup71190: i am not counting on anything

buttercup71190: wow

buttercup71190: i think "Design-a-Site" is involved

mrmagoo7: won't know any of that for a while yet, they just had the grand jury *inditement* last week, more will come from this

buttercup71190: i am sure

buttercup71190: USATODAY.com—FBI online sex stings winning first convictions

. . . Feds indict 19 on online ID theft charges—2:29 AM . . . "It's a growth business, which is scary," said Dooley, who heads Connecticut's cybercrime unit . . .

www.usatoday.com/tech/news/2004-01-25-pedo-stings_x.htm

mrmagoo7: loading

buttercup71190: go to altavista to do search then type in

buttercup71190: feds indict cybercrime id theft

buttercup71190: lots of news results

mrmagoo7: you got mail

mrmagoo7: http://www.net-intrusion.com/member/data/arrest_info.html

mrmagoo7: not related, just weird

buttercup71190: k

buttercup71190: btw

buttercup71190: thank your friends for me

mrmagoo7: done!

buttercup71190: already?

buttercup71190: wow ur efficient

mrmagoo7: its posted, waiting for a reply

buttercup71190: k

mrmagoo7: they should be on later this week, they said something about a break after the election

buttercup71190: cool

buttercup71190: did u tell them when i had trouble with the id theft?

mrmagoo7: yes

buttercup71190: oh ok

buttercup71190: i thought maybe you thought it was not related

mrmagoo7: i gave them all the info on that anyway

mrmagoo7: http://www.classesusa.com/featuredschools/programs/featured_criminal.cap

mrmagoo7: this is right up your alley, lol

buttercup71190: what are you trying to tell me?

mrmagoo7: might as well get a degree, its a start, hee hee

buttercup71190: maybe they'll give me a scholarship

mrmagoo7: lol

buttercup71190: maybe i can skip the education and get the job

buttercup71190: lol

buttercup71190: internet forensics

mrmagoo7: there ya go

buttercup71190: not computer but internet forensics

mrmagoo7: they are always lookin

mrmagoo7: you off tomorrow?

buttercup71190: yes

mrmagoo7:　　　　bout friggin time, lol

buttercup71190: lol

mrmagoo7:　　　　http://www.usatoday.com/tech/
news/computersecurity/2004-09-20-
cybersleuths_x.htm

mrmagoo7:　　　　you gotta read this

buttercup71190: k

mrmagoo7:　　　　still want the job?, lol

buttercup71190: lol

buttercup71190: yea

buttercup71190: those reward funds look interesting

buttercup71190: lol

mrmagoo7:　　　　yeah really

buttercup71190: i wonder how much the credit card
companies would put up

buttercup71190: During Justice's recent investigation,
the NCFTA discovered through industry
experts that hundreds of powerful
computers at the Defense Department
and U.S. Senate were hijacked by
hackers

buttercup71190: now doesn't that make u feel safe? LOL

mrmagoo7:　　　　but of course

mrmagoo7:　　　　lol

mrmagoo7:　　　　Consumers and businesses, as a
consequence, lost at least $14 billion
to digital thieves last year, although
most of the crimes went undetected
or unreported, experts say.

buttercup71190: wow

mrmagoo7:　　　　In an attack in the USA last month,
the Web site of Authorize.Net, a
processor of credit card transactions
for thousands of small and midsize

businesses, was hit for several days, disrupting service. Authorize.Net rejected several e-mails demanding a "significant amount" of money, says David Schwartz, a spokesman. An unknown number of zombie computers were used in the attack, he said. The FBI is investigating.

mrmagoo7: Authorize.Net downplayed the attacks, but some of its customers said the withering assaults were costly. "I lost $15,000," says David Hoekje, president of PartsGuy.com, an online retailer of heating and air-conditioning parts.

buttercup71190: i wonder if it was related to my case.

buttercup71190: they did the same thing to "Design-a-Site" when i was with them

buttercup71190: then authorize ✒

mrmagoo7: yup

buttercup71190: what site did u read that at?

mrmagoo7: http://www.usatoday.com/tech/news/2004-10-20-cyber-crime_x.htm

mrmagoo7: quite the *artical*

buttercup71190: what are dos attacks?

mrmagoo7: denial of service attacks

buttercup71190: what does that mean?

buttercup71190: i knew that

mrmagoo7: they attack the servers so that they cannot *proccess* orders

buttercup71190: oh

buttercup71190: and refunds wouldn't get processed?

mrmagoo7: some will even *proccess* the orders to diverted accounts mrmagoo7:   exactly

buttercup71190: oh

buttercup71190: i guess these guys are pissed at me

mrmagoo7:   Another popular scam entails an elaborate shipping network for expensive goods purchased online with stolen credit cards. Fraudulent online buyers in West Africa have goods shipped to Europe, where an accomplice or legitimate delivery service re-ships the items to West Africa, FBI agents say. Re-shippers are recruited in chat rooms, online job postings and over the phone. They are either paid with counterfeit cashier's checks or allowed to keep some merchandise. Though the scheme requires a cash outlay, it is an inexpensive way to move stolen products without revealing the identity of the original buyer, agents say.

Working with the FBI, Nigerian officials recently seized more than $340,000 in illegally obtained online merchandise and recovered $115,000 in fraudulent cashier's checks is

mrmagoo7:   yes just a little, lol

buttercup71190: lol

buttercup71190: u think they know i was behind it?

buttercup71190: and u?

mrmagoo7:   ohnonononono, ummmmmmmmmmmm yes

buttercup71190: ?

mrmagoo7:   they know you didnt help em any, lol

buttercup71190: yes or no

buttercup71190: lol

buttercup71190: i think they wanted me to go away

mrmagoo7:   thats putting it politely, lol

buttercup71190: my mom is nervous for me

buttercup71190: she thinks they will retaliate

mrmagoo7:   she shouldnt be

buttercup71190: that's what i told her

mrmagoo7:   its not the local schmuck cops dealing with these guys, it's the FBI and the secret service

buttercup71190: so what does that mean for me?

mrmagoo7:   even when they are out they will be watched like a rat runnin through a cathouse

buttercup71190: k

buttercup71190: that's what i thought

mrmagoo7:   every phone call they ever make will be monitored and every conversation will be listened in on

buttercup71190: read this http://news.yahoo.com/fc?t mpl=fc&cid=34&in=tech&cat=cybercr ime_and_internet_fraud

mrmagoo7:   k

buttercup71190: http://www.ftc.gov/opa/2004/10/ spyware.htm

buttercup71190: that is the full article

buttercup71190: need to log off now

buttercup71190: need to scan my puter

mrmagoo7:   k

mrmagoo7:   lol

buttercup71190: got something installed

mrmagoo7:   gettin nervous after reading all this shit?

mrmagoo7:   what?

buttercup71190: no

buttercup71190: vcom picked up something

buttercup71190: u can call

mrmagoo7:   oh ok

buttercup71190: bye for now

mrmagoo7:   k

November 4, 2004

buttercup71190: http://news.zdnet.
co.uk/0,39020330,39171958,00.htm

mrmagoo7:   probably garys cousin, lol

buttercup71190: lol

buttercup71190: "[The group] compromised bank accounts from hacking, phishing and other means of fraud,"

buttercup71190: Police investigated online forums, which led them to arrest 28 suspects and discover a Bulgarian passport forging facility.

mrmagoo7:   cool

buttercup71190: yea

mrmagoo7:   no wonder the secret service was involved

buttercup71190: the whole id theft went overseas anyway

buttercup71190: that was just frosting on the cake

buttercup71190: lol

buttercup71190: a bonus

buttercup71190: thank you!

mrmagoo7:   you are most welcome!

buttercup71190: http://money.cnn.com/2004/08/26/ technology/cybercrime/index. htm?cnn=yes

buttercup71190: 53 convictions involving a series of cyber crimes that targeted 150,000 victims.

mrmagoo7: yep, thats them, lol

buttercup71190: Justice Department officials said victims lost more than $215 million.

mrmagoo7: Department officials said victims lost more than $215 million.

mrmagoo7: lmao

buttercup71190: lol

mrmagoo7: there is only enough room in my head for one of us, lol

buttercup71190: lol

mrmagoo7: The Federal Trade Commission says 10 million Americans had their identities stolen last year. The Justice Department says identity theft costs the nation's businesses nearly $50 billion a year in fraudulent transactions.

buttercup71190: i know

buttercup71190: http://www.geek.com/ news/geeknews/2004Nov/ gee20041101027651.htm

mrmagoo7: http://www.cybertelecom.org/security/ crime.htm

buttercup71190: Wake-UP & Read Between The Lines!! (5:01pm EST Wed Nov 03 2004)

This case is a lot more then credit cards, hmmmm . . . . counterfeit passports, counterfeit drivers licenses, counterfeit diplomas, etc. "hackers for hire" (Title 18 USC 1030), Identity Theft, money laundering, International Organized Crime (US & Russian Forums swapping criminal activity), ehm—PhreekR who's side you on? When people like you become victims, then all they do is scream that the government is not doing enough. Are you a victim of the Patriot Act???? I think not, otherwise it would be all over the news. Outstanding job by the USSS & the International Community! International borders are transparent to organized criminals. Law enforcement agencies must respect international borders & not infringe on them.

buttercup71190: However, in this case it is very apparent that law enforcement worked across these lines in a highly technical manner & got the bad guys! "You are No Longer Anonymous!!" Bad Guys: Enjoy your time, while I enjoy my freedom!!!—by Conscious Citizen

mrmagoo7: lolol

mrmagoo7: perfect!

buttercup71190: lol

buttercup71190: it's happened before, never of this magnitude, but they'll be back. They were 4000 strong. At the most 100 will be arrested, charged, and found guilty. They just went after the admins and mods, the vendors and the high profile guys. The only reason they caught who they did is because they got sloppy.

mrmagoo7:   yes read that and guess what, they are dead wrong on this one

buttercup71190:   ?

mrmagoo7:   well first off they will get just about everyone involved, not just a 100 or so . . . .

buttercup71190:   ok

mrmagoo7:   and second, there wont be anything left to re-open

buttercup71190:   The operation began in November 2003 after credit card company MasterCard International briefed law enforcement agents on more than 100 Web sites and Internet chat rooms that specialize in credit card and identity document trafficking.

mrmagoo7:   and 3rd, no-one would be so stupid as to try it again

buttercup71190:   lol

mrmagoo7:   gonna post your comment?

buttercup71190:   what comment?

mrmagoo7:   you can post a comment on the bottom of the page

buttercup71190:   yes what comment?

mrmagoo7:   anything you want!, lol

buttercup71190:   u post it for me

mrmagoo7:   within reason of course

buttercup71190:   lol

mrmagoo7:   have to be careful what is said

mrmagoo7:   dont want em knockin on our doors, lol

buttercup71190:   who?

mrmagoo7:   sec serv

buttercup71190:   lol

buttercup71190: they already know who i am

buttercup71190: u can post something for me just tell me what you posted

mrmagoo7: i could easily get ten years if i piss em off

buttercup71190: lol

buttercup71190: http://www.ustreas.gov/usss/press/ pub2304.pdf

mrmagoo7: yeah i'd say i can hang up my tights now, lol

buttercup71190: lol

buttercup71190: additional info is available at the US district court of NJ

mrmagoo7: cool

mrmagoo7: http://pacer.njd.uscourts.gov/

buttercup71190: The Bulgarian counterfeit master of Bill Gates-card has played a crucial role in the international cyber gang busted in seven countries earlier this week.

buttercup71190: The 22-aged Aleksey has been arrested

buttercup71190: http://www.novinite.com/view_news. php?id=40933

buttercup71190: A 19-year-old man from Camberley, Surrey, was arrested by the National Hi-Tech Crime Unit but has been bailed.

buttercup71190: The authorities in the US, who have indicted 19 people in Newark, New Jersey, estimate the fraud caused losses of more than $4m.

mrmagoo7: i haven't heard about anyone else *bein* bailed and i don't think they will *buttercup71190:*   http://news.bbc.co.uk/nolpda/ukfs_news/hi/newsid_3965000/3965975.stm

buttercup71190:   The US Secret Service was first tipped off in July 2003

buttercup71190:   wonder who tipped them off? lol

mrmagoo7:   gee i wouldnt know

buttercup71190:   lol

buttercup71190:   interesting article

buttercup71190:   The activities at Cruising-the-Shadows were profiled in a September 2002 internetnews.com story The Great Credit Card Bazaar.

buttercup71190:   http://www.internetnews.com/ec-news/article.php/1467331

mrmagoo7:   We have a couple of undercover operations working," said Don Masters, head of a Secret Service high-tech crime unit in Los Angeles. "We jump into these cases. We look at those that are a threat to the nation's banking and financing infrastructure."

mrmagoo7:   havin connection trouble?

buttercup71190:   lol

buttercup71190:   yea with some of these sites

buttercup71190:   The family that spams together gets sent to the can together.

A Virginia jury has recommended a nine-year jail sentence for 30-year-old spammer Jeremy and a $7,500 fine for his 28-year-old sister Jessica. Sounds like they got the fuzzy end of that lollipop, yikes.

The pair were convicted on three felony counts of spam, the first to enjoy that honor. Prosecutors say the duo were "modern-day snake oil salesmen" who amassed $24 million via bogus schemes such as a work-at-home "FedEx refund processor" gig, a "penny stock picker" and an Internet history eraser.

Their lawyer is trying to fight the nine-year sentence, saying it was excessive when compared to those for violent crimes.

mrmagoo7:	nail em
buttercup71190:	lol
mrmagoo7:	what do you say we go back to stoning, lol
mrmagoo7:	get your rocks handy
buttercup71190:	lol
mrmagoo7:	http://lawlibrary.rutgers.edu/fed/search.html
buttercup71190:	http://www.technewsworld.com/story/37731.html
buttercup71190:	The members, who were vetted in an attempt to keep out law enforcement, communicated through private forums and chat rooms, where they offered raw information or counterfeit documents for sale and posted hacking methods and other illicit information. Counterfeit Euros and passports were also found during one of the arrests.
mrmagoo7:	oops, lol
buttercup71190:	lol
buttercup71190:	The Secret Service used wiretaps, an undercover informant and their own

hackers to gain access to the private portions of the site.

mrmagoo7:

guess they were in the wrong forums, lol . . . . too bad for them the forum we use is much more exclusive

buttercup71190: lol

mrmagoo7: that would be us,

buttercup71190: An access device can be anything from credit cards and their account numbers to debit cards and their personal identification numbers (PINs), ATM cards and their PINs, computer passwords, long-distance access codes, and the computer chips in cellular phones that assign billing—in other words, anything that leads to the access of financial information.

buttercup71190: The U.K. National Hi-Tech Crimes Unit, the Royal Canadian Mounted Police and Europol were among the agencies in on the investigation. American Express (NYSE: AXP), Discover, Mastercard and Visa were also involved.

buttercup71190: how come they are taking credit now? saying it was going on longer when it started in July 2003?

mrmagoo7: they are the heaviest charges against em and carry the largest fines and sentences

buttercup71190: Nagel stressed that cooperation among the agencies and credit card companies was key. About 90 percent of the arrests were made within an hour of each other to prevent the word from spreading and giving suspects time to encrypt or destroy information.

mrmagoo7: this did not start out as a fraud investigation but after so much information was retrieved and all these agencies pooled their info together they found something larger

buttercup71190: http://www.technewsworld.com/story/37731.html

buttercup71190: Man gets probation after admitting to Net stalking

A South Carolina man who pleaded guilty to two counts of breaking a federal Internet stalking law was sentenced Friday to five years of probation, 500 hours of community service and more than $12,000 in restitution. James Robert, 38, of Columbia, S.C., admitted sending dozens of e-mails and faxes to Seattle city employee Joelle, who broke up with him about 14 years ago

buttercup71190: dont laugh too hard

mrmagoo7: well there isnt much else to do in sc, lol

buttercup71190: lol

buttercup71190: here you go all the info!!!

http://www.usdoj.gov/usao/nj/publicaffairs/NJ_Press/files/pdffiles/firewallindct1028.pdf

mrmagoo7: loading

buttercup71190: all the names

mrmagoo7: cool beans

buttercup71190: yep

buttercup71190: a lot of reading here

buttercup71190: lol

mrmagoo7: yes i know

mrmagoo7:   more than a few italian names

buttercup71190: lol

buttercup71190: yeah

buttercup71190: Mandel

buttercup71190: and rocknrollforever

mrmagoo7:   Andrew rings a bell

buttercup71190: who is that?

mrmagoo7:   not sure, i will have to boot killer up
                   and look

mrmagoo7:   but that name stands out for some
                   reason

buttercup71190: was that one of the puters u were in?

mrmagoo7:   i'm not sure, but that name stands
                   out, way out

buttercup71190: did u encrypt any info in any of the
                   machines?

buttercup71190: so they could not erase it?

mrmagoo7:   part of the drives on the machines we
                   went into are hidden and protected
                   from their owners

mrmagoo7:   i'm sure the FBI found it though

mrmagoo7:   we copied info from their machines
                   into a hidden partition on each drive
                   for each machine

buttercup71190: oh ok

mrmagoo7:   it sounds complicated, but it's pretty
                   simple, only takes about ten minutes
                   to do

buttercup71190: k

buttercup71190: Rbot-GR, the latest variant of a prolific
                   worm series, exploits a number of
                   Microsoft security vulnerabilities
                   to drop a backdoor Trojan horse

program on vulnerable machines as it propagates The Register reports.

Rbot-GR comes pre-loaded with functionality specifically designed to control webcams and microphones.

"If your computer is infected and you have a webcam plugged in, then everything you do in front of the computer can be seen, and everything you say can be recorded," said Graham, senior technology consultant for AV firm Sophos.

Aside from its voyeuristic *behaviour*, the Trojan component of the worm will attempt to steal registration information for games and PayPal passwords from infected machines.

mrmagoo7:	Rbot-GR was in my update signature list on vcom

November 5, 2004

buttercup71190:	i wonder if someone was following that guy and switched the bags then turned it in
mrmagoo7:	don't know, but those docs are gonna turn up everywhere
mrmagoo7:	they are worth gold
buttercup71190:	where will they turn up?
mrmagoo7:	all over the world
buttercup71190:	from Cruising-the-Shadows members?
mrmagoo7:	i dont even know who created em
mrmagoo7:	yes they came from Cruising-the-Shadows

buttercup71190: k

buttercup71190: sounds bizarre that someone just left them at a bus stop though

mrmagoo7: yeah very strange and the timing sucks, lol

buttercup71190: lol

buttercup71190: maybe one of his "friends" turned them in

buttercup71190: for a lighter sentence lol

mrmagoo7: who knows

mrmagoo7: sounds more like one of his friends stole em out of the guys house for police and met them at the bus stop

buttercup71190: that's what i said lol

mrmagoo7: i said it more better

buttercup71190: lol

buttercup71190: http://www.wired.com/news/privacy/0,1848,56567,00.html

buttercup71190: Posing as employees of those companies, the criminals would then obtain and download customer credit records, which contain sensitive information such as bank account and credit card data as well as Social Security numbers.

These records were then sold to a network of thieves who used them to drain bank accounts, open new lines of credit, order new checkbooks and other activities.

mrmagoo7: reading

mrmagoo7: all this is stemming from the same investigation, gonna be reading about a lot more of this for months

buttercup71190: that what i was thinking

buttercup71190: alot of arrests

mrmagoo7: do you see how much havoc you have caused, on a global scale yet, i hope you are happy with yourself young lady, lol

buttercup71190: lol who me?

mrmagoo7: and i thought you were such a nice quiet person, lol

mrmagoo7: bet you had no idea it would lead to all this, i know i didnt

buttercup71190: didnt think it was this big

buttercup71190: http://www.wcow.com/html/internet_fraud.html

mrmagoo7: the internet is now your gotham city

buttercup71190: lol

buttercup71190: tell catwoman

mrmagoo7: you tell her, you live closer

buttercup71190: lol

mrmagoo7: purrrrrrrrrrrrrrrrrr

buttercup71190: that link i just sent has a lot of links about internet fraud recently concluded

mrmagoo7: yes i seen that

buttercup71190: http://home.rica.net/alphae/419coal/news2004.htm

buttercup71190: Before the court are 65-year-old Patricia, who faces 89 charges of fraud, forgery and theft, and her 78-year-old aunt, Elva Mary, accused of two charges of theft.

mrmagoo7: rica.net?

buttercup71190: yea lol

mrmagoo7:   http://story.news.yahoo.com/news?tmpl=story&u=/pcworld/20041104/tc_pcworld/118446&e=11&ncid=1093

buttercup71190:   http://waysandmeans.house.gov/media/pdf/ss/factsfigures.pdf

mrmagoo7:   hey i can use this for my web site ty

buttercup71190:   lol

mrmagoo7:   btw . . . .

mrmagoo7:   i just got a message on the message board

mrmagoo7:   want a look at your new friends

mrmagoo7:   this is where they work, they gave me the addy

mrmagoo7:   or have been working since the war started anyway

mrmagoo7:   https://www.it-isac.org/

mrmagoo7:   now i know exactly how the info got to the right people

buttercup71190:   lol

buttercup71190:   wow

buttercup71190:   impressive

buttercup71190:   do they have any openings/

mrmagoo7:   whats your security clearance, lol

buttercup71190:   i dont know ask them

mrmagoo7:   i should be gettin an email soon from them if i got a message on the board

buttercup71190:   what did they say?

mrmagoo7:   just told me "watch the news, keep my eyes open and check out this site"

buttercup71190:   k

buttercup71190: u cant access any other pages though

mrmagoo7: they have membership levels: https://www.it-isac.org/showmatrix. php

buttercup71190: u a member?

mrmagoo7: https://www.it-isac.org/membershipreq. php

mrmagoo7: not yet

mrmagoo7: i didnt even know about it til a half hour ago, lol

buttercup71190: lol

buttercup71190: so y didnt u join yet?

buttercup71190: i think i got your friends some really good jobs

mrmagoo7: yeah sure, look at the rates, lol

buttercup71190: guess we wont be a member for a while

buttercup71190: we should get a free membership after everything we did lol

mrmagoo7: yeah right, lol

buttercup71190: your friends got a good job out of this

mrmagoo7: they didnt get their jobs because of the hackers, they used their jobs to get info of the hackers to the right people

buttercup71190: yes i know

mrmagoo7: are you gettin kicked again?

buttercup71190: yep lol

mrmagoo7: well knock it off

buttercup71190: lol

mrmagoo7: gives me a headache, lol

buttercup71190: wonder what's going to show up on that site *buttercup71190:* the one your friends told u to watch

mrmagoo7: oh i dont know

mrmagoo7: i'm gonna sign up as a free member

buttercup71190: The software company took issue with the public release of the vulnerability before it had been notified.

buttercup71190: Microsoft has begun to investigate the Iframe vulnerability and has not been made aware of any program designed to exploit the flaw, the company said in an email statement to ZDNet UK sister site CNET News.com.

mrmagoo7: hmmmmmm

buttercup71190: The US watchdog for Internet threats, the Computer Emergency Readiness Team (CERT), has also warned government and industry users about the Iframe flaw.

mrmagoo7: oh yeah?

buttercup71190: The US-CERT alert notes that other programs using the WebBrowser Active X control, could be affected by the vulnerability. These programs include Microsoft's Outlook and Outlook Express, America Online's browser, and Lotus Notes.

buttercup71190: http://news.zdnet. co.uk/0,39020330,39172736,00.htm here read the article in full

buttercup71190: i'd make a good analyst

mrmagoo7: yeah i'd say so

buttercup71190: Several vulnerabilities exist in the Mozilla web browser and derived products, the most serious of which could allow a remote attacker to execute arbitrary code on an affected system.

buttercup71190: These vulnerabilities could allow a remote attacker to execute arbitrary code with the privileges of the user running the affected application.

VU#847200 could also allow a remote attacker to crash an affected application.

buttercup71190: Affected Versions:

* Mozilla web browser, email and newsgroup client

* Firefox web browser

* Thunderbird email client

buttercup71190: https://www.it-isac.org/postings/cyber/alertdetail.php?id=2539

buttercup71190: that's the link to the info

mrmagoo7: oh friggin wonderful

buttercup71190: lol

buttercup71190: just for u

mrmagoo7: is there a patch?

buttercup71190: they tell u all the code and what it does

mrmagoo7: k, ty

buttercup71190: Upgrade to a patched version

Mozilla has released versions of the affected software that contain patches for these issues:

* Mozilla 1.7.3

* Firefox Preview Release

* Thunderbird 0.8

mrmagoo7: i quit!, lol

buttercup71190: go to that link i sent

mrmagoo7: i'm there, my version is unaffected it says, thank god

buttercup71190: lol

buttercup71190: microsoft has some major updating to security to do

buttercup71190: https://www.it-isac.org/postings/cyber/alerts.php

mrmagoo7: oh btw, dont put service pack 2 on any more machines, it's been compromized

mrmagoo7: hackers have a back door into it

buttercup71190: gee ty

mrmagoo7: w

buttercup71190: i have it on mine

mrmagoo7: is it on yours?

buttercup71190: yes

mrmagoo7: uninstall it

mrmagoo7: i just read it today in pc magazine

buttercup71190: but then service pack one is not good either

mrmagoo7: no, service pack one is ok

buttercup71190: not according to this site

mrmagoo7: service pack one has been patched with the critical updates, serv pack 2 has not

December 31, 2004

buttercup71190: did u see your friends on the other day?

mrmagoo7: no but i got an email

buttercup71190: oh and?

mrmagoo7:	it said all is well in hackland and i should be recieving some documents in the mail soon
mrmagoo7:	dont know what yet though
buttercup71190:	documents? hmmmmmmmmmm
mrmagoo7:	beats me lol
buttercup71190:	cool
buttercup71190:	now i am curious
buttercup71190:	tell them i cant wait hurry up lol
mrmagoo7:	they said they ran some intercepts on your machine too recently
buttercup71190:	intercepts?
mrmagoo7:	yeah dont know what thats about either
buttercup71190:	something was trying to come in?
mrmagoo7:	i guess, they stopped it
buttercup71190:	i'm so glad they are watching my machine
mrmagoo7:	like a hawk
buttercup71190:	i think i have pissed a bunch of people off
mrmagoo7:	well between you and i, they ran some traces on your phone too
buttercup71190:	cool
buttercup71190:	and?
mrmagoo7:	dont know
buttercup71190:	ohhhhhhhhh
buttercup71190:	did u ever get my mom's email?
mrmagoo7:	over the past 6 mos they said
buttercup71190:	ok
mrmagoo7:	which email?
buttercup71190:	maybe that was them we heard on the phone
mrmagoo7:	possibly

buttercup71190:   the email about the phone problems recently

mrmagoo7:   nope

buttercup71190:   she told me she emailed you

mrmagoo7:   when?

buttercup71190:   about a week or so

mrmagoo7:   i'll check again when i get home

mrmagoo7:   might be on my server

mrmagoo7:   what are you up to over there?

mrmagoo7:   and wheres my pics damn it, lol

mrmagoo7:   sorry i had to rebbot

mrmagoo7:   missed the last couple of lines

mrmagoo7:   reboot

mrmagoo7:   YOU THERE?

mrmagoo7:   you hoo

  BUZZ!!!

  mrmagoo7 has signed back in. (12/31/2004 6:16 PM)

buttercup71190:   ib

buttercup71190:   had to tend to my guests

mrmagoo7:   oh thought you were mad at me again, lol

mrmagoo7:   wb

buttercup71190:   no sorry had to help them

buttercup71190:   the one guy here looks like mikejoe

mrmagoo7:   really?

mrmagoo7:   act like him?

buttercup71190:   i only had a pic of him and i dont know what he really looks like. but this guy looks like the pic

buttercup71190:   everytime i look at him it reminds me of him mrmagoo7: you dont think its him do ya?

buttercup71190: the guy here with the Russian group is not Russian

buttercup71190: so i am not sure

buttercup71190: he has a girlfriend with him too

mrmagoo7: i dont think they would pull that, not now

buttercup71190: dont know

buttercup71190: i hope not

buttercup71190: anytime i rent now i am somewhat nervous. not sure who might be sent here to spy on me lol

buttercup71190: hackers friends or neighbor's friend

buttercup71190: i hope my internet store takes off

buttercup71190: then i wouldnt have to rent

buttercup71190: and worry

mrmagoo7: it will and its all fixed now

buttercup71190: cool

mrmagoo7: shouldnt be any more problems with it now

buttercup71190: maybe i made "Design-a-Site" mad at me

mrmagoo7: oh well, lol

buttercup71190: maybe i hit the nail on the head

buttercup71190: did ur friends say when u will get the info

mrmagoo7: nope

mrmagoo7: just said they were sending me some documents

mrmagoo7: didnt say when or what

buttercup71190: y not?

buttercup71190: tell them to hurry up

buttercup71190: i'm dying to know

mrmagoo7:   cause they just like making me wonder, it gives them pleasure, lol

buttercup71190: i really want this to end

mrmagoo7:   well its basically ended already, just gonna take some time for the dust to settle

buttercup71190: i heard they are all out on bond

mrmagoo7:   yeah bond is only temporary my dear

buttercup71190: arent they being watched?

buttercup71190: while out

mrmagoo7:   but of course

buttercup71190: were they all arrested?

mrmagoo7:   as far as i know, yes

buttercup71190: cool

buttercup71190: can i visit them in jail to see for myself?

buttercup71190: lol

mrmagoo7:   yes i'll drive you

buttercup71190: ok cool when?

mrmagoo7:   when they get sentenced

buttercup71190: that's a long time from now

mrmagoo7:   not necessarily

buttercup71190: u think soon?

mrmagoo7:   probly a few months is all

buttercup71190: WOW

mrmagoo7:   thats not too bad

April 12, 2005

mrmagoo7 appears to be offline
and will receive your messages after signing in.

buttercup71190: breaking news

buttercup71190: http://www.channelregister.
co.uk/2005/03/23/id_theft_cannot_
be_escaped/

buttercup71190: http://www.cbsnews.com/
stories/2005/03/10/tech/main679237.
shtml

buttercup71190: "This is wholesale theft of consumer
data and there is almost nothing
individuals can do to prevent this
type of hacking."

buttercup71190: http://www.washingtonpost.com/
wp-dyn/articles/A19982-2005Mar9.
html

buttercup71190: http://forums.thelaw.com/archive/
index.php/t-4416.html

buttercup71190: http://www.computerworld.com/
securitytopics/security/hacking/
story/0,10801,96900,00.html

buttercup71190: http://netscape.com.com/
ID-theft+alert+follows+break-
in+at+federal+contractor/2100-1029_3-
5575861.html

buttercup71190: http://forums.net-integration.net/index.
php?s=53321815509b40012c9925f72d
7088b9&showtopic=29406&st=0&#en
try140206

buttercup71190: http://www.megasecurity.org/News/
News112000.html

buttercup71190: http://www.securityawareness.com/
secnews.htm

buttercup71190: 19 March 2005—Computer Stolen
from Nevada DMV Contains Motorist
Data

Thieves broke into a Nevada Department
of Motor Vehicles office and stole a

computer that contains personal data belonging to more than 8,900 licensed Nevada drivers. The information includes names, birth dates, Social Security numbers, photographs and signatures. The Nevada DMV initially said the data was encrypted, but DMV chief Ginny Lewis said the company that makes the state's digital driver's licenses told her the data was not encrypted. All Nevada DMV licensing stations have been ordered to remove personal information from computers; the department plans to send letters to the people whose data is on the stolen computer. In addition to the computer, the thieves also stole 1,700 blank licenses and the equipment to make licenses. The US Secret Service is investigating.

buttercup71190: Operation Higher Education

buttercup71190: Operation Digital Gridlock

buttercup71190: http://www.iasoc.net/news.htm

buttercup71190: OPERATION CANDY BOX

buttercup71190: OPERATION STRAIGHT ID

buttercup71190: http://www.reviewjournal.com/lvrj_home/2005/Apr-08-Fri-2005/news/26246116.html

buttercup71190: http://www.tecrime.com/llartF02.htm

buttercup71190: Operation Tarmac

buttercup71190: http://www.news-record.com/news/local/gso/arrests_030905.htm

buttercup71190: http://www.ice.gov/text/news/factsheets/worksite031805.htm

buttercup71190: Operation Glow Worm

buttercup71190: Operation Safe Cities

buttercup71190: Operation Rollback

buttercup71190: an investigation focused on violations at Wal-Mart retail stores throughout the United States, targeting illegal aliens working for cleaning contractors employed at the stores.

buttercup71190: lol

buttercup71190: operation Twilight

buttercup71190: operation Breakthrough

May 1, 2005

mrmagoo7 appears to be offline
and will receive your messages after signing in.

buttercup71190: http://www.virus.org/Article74.html

buttercup71190: http://www.4law.co.il/jacob1.htm

buttercup71190: http://www.e-evidence.info/205.html read the last link

buttercup71190: State of NY sues spyware firm

New York State Attorney General Eliot Spitzer has announced a lawsuit against Los Angeles-based Intermix Media, Inc. According to the AG's press release, the company is allegedly responsible for not only secretly downloading spyware to victim PCs, but no uninstaller was provided and the programs sometimes "reinstalled themselves after being deleted."

buttercup71190: http://antivirus.about.com/b/archives.htm

buttercup71190: http://cryptogon.com/2005_03_27_
blogarchive.html

buttercup71190: In a high-profile investigation last fall,
code-named "Operation Firewall,"
Secret Service agents infiltrated an
Internet crime ring used to buy and
sell stolen credit cards, a case that
yielded more than 30 arrests but also
huge amounts of encrypted data. DNA
is still toiling to crack most of those
codes, many of which were created
with a formidable grade of 256-bit
encryption

buttercup71190: The Secret Service also is working on
adapting DNA to cope with emergent
data secrecy threats, such as an increased
criminal use of "steganography,"
which involves hiding information
by embedding messages inside other,
seemingly innocuous messages, music
files or images.

buttercup71190: http://www.privacydigest.com/topic/
hmmm/2005/03/30.html

buttercup71190: The Secret Service has deployed DNA
to 40 percent of its internal computers
at a rate of a few PCs per week
and plans to expand the program
to all 10,000 of its systems by the
end of this summer. Ultimately, the
agency hopes to build the network
out across all 22 federal agencies
that comprise the Department of
Homeland Security: It currently holds
a license to deploy the network out
to 100,000 systems.

buttercup71190: new news today

buttercup71190: http://www.usatoday.com/printedition/ news/20050429/a_licenses29.art.htm

buttercup71190: Florida driver's licenses figured in the terrorist attacks of Sept. 11. Nine of the 19 hijackers held Florida licenses and three others had identification cards issued by Florida.

Buttercup71190: Operation Cornerstone, run by the Bureau of Immigration and Customs Enforcement (ICE), is a new financial investigations program that will identify vulnerabilities in financial systems through which criminals launder their illicit proceeds, bring the criminals to justice and work to eliminate the vulnerabilities.

buttercup71190: These task forces investigate a wide range of computer-based criminal activity. Examples include e-commerce frauds, identity crimes, telecommunications fraud, and a wide variety of computer intrusion crimes that affect a variety of infrastructures.

buttercup71190: Last year the Secret Service arrested 1143 people for violations involving credit card or access device fraud.

buttercup71190: http://mensnewsdaily.com/blog/kouri/ archive/2005_03_01_archive.html

buttercup71190: did u see the world news tonight?

mrmagoo7:   no, been working all day, finally decided to quit

buttercup71190: i found one link for a similar story that i sent as an offline message

mrmagoo7:   what was on the news?

buttercup71190: http://www.usatoday.com/printedition/ news/20050429/a_licenses29.art.htm *buttercup71190:* about the license scams

buttercup71190: and 9/11

mrmagoo7:   reading

mrmagoo7:   wow thats just coming out on the news now?

buttercup71190: yes

mrmagoo7:   thats been on the message board for months

buttercup71190: i know

buttercup71190: but a few weeks ago they told you to watch the news

mrmagoo7:   yepper

mrmagoo7:   big story now, lol

buttercup71190: i have been finding that the stories on the internet are out about a month or two before its on tv

mrmagoo7:   yepper

buttercup71190: this story is dated yesterday

buttercup71190: was on nbc tonight

mrmagoo7:   i have got to get these security protocols right on here before wedsday

mrmagoo7:   i may have to wipe this xp out and put win 2000 pro back on here

buttercup71190: oh

mrmagoo7:   cant seem to get it to work on xp

buttercup71190: or maybe send them an e-mail

mrmagoo7:   thats why i never installed it on my main machine and only the laptop

mrmagoo7:   i've already sent em emails

buttercup71190: any response?

mrmagoo7:   just one last week

buttercup71190: i am anxious to find out what is going on

mrmagoo7: well i doubt that we will hear anything much this soon

mrmagoo7: but i'll keep trying anyway

buttercup71190: i just want to know how close they are to finishing up with the hackers

buttercup71190: id thieves

mrmagoo7: well i broke their whole case for 'em and they haven't told me much of anything yet

mrmagoo7: and its all your fault, lol

buttercup71190: y not? tell them inquiring minds need to know

buttercup71190: me?

mrmagoo7: yes its your fault i went in there and found the shit in the first place, lol

buttercup71190: right after i told u what i suspected?

mrmagoo7: no when i finally broke into those machines to get the evidence

buttercup71190: that was after i thought my id was stolen?

mrmagoo7: what are you doing?

buttercup71190: clicking on some links i should not

buttercup71190: by accident

mrmagoo7: oh dont do that

mrmagoo7: you got 2 orders this month?

buttercup71190: yes

mrmagoo7: cool

buttercup71190: from the old catalog lol

mrmagoo7: been getting all your mail?

buttercup71190: the new one just came out. i think so

mrmagoo7: can you still fill the orders?

buttercup71190: i need to check on this last one

buttercup71190: btw . .

buttercup71190: i am going to send u all the pics once i have them scanned in to resize for me

mrmagoo7: ok

buttercup71190: i just need to vent

mrmagoo7: np on the venting, vent anytime

buttercup71190: lol

mrmagoo7: brb, i need a drink

buttercup71190: have one for me lol

buttercup71190: Time, Event, Intruder, Count

4/30/2005 11:41:18 PM, SQL_SSRP_ Slammer_Worm, 1

4/30/2005 11:41:18 PM, SQL_SSRP_ StackBo, 1

mrmagoo7: oh i dont know, i havent talked to anyone in like two weeks

buttercup71190: and what did they say about that the last time?

mrmagoo7: not much

mrmagoo7: last time i talked to anyone was to let em know i was leaving florida

buttercup71190: i'm logging off soon

buttercup71190: i'll be on for a bit

mrmagoo7: oh ok

mrmagoo7: cool

mrmagoo7: gonna setup my desk and puker

buttercup71190: cool

mrmagoo7: bout time right, lol

mrmagoo7: gonna setup killer too

buttercup71190: good

mrmagoo7: gonna wipe her out soon too

mrmagoo7: poor baby

buttercup71190: y?

buttercup71190: u cant

buttercup71190: kill her

mrmagoo7: she has no other programs or purpose

mrmagoo7: and thanks to you it's getting quite dangerous to hack anymore

mrmagoo7: ya meany, lol

buttercup71190: lol

buttercup71190: ethical hacking is ok though

mrmagoo7: sure, i got lucky this time

mrmagoo7: i could have ended up spending the next 20 years in federal court, lol

buttercup71190: well u should not have put yourself on the line then. u did not tell me what you were doing

mrmagoo7: too bad

mrmagoo7: i knew the risks

mrmagoo7: it was about time somebody stood up for you, i'm glad i was able to do just that

buttercup71190: ty for believing in me

mrmagoo7: you are quite welcome my dear, i would do it again without hesitation

mrmagoo7: i told you right away if i could do anything i would

buttercup71190: ty

buttercup71190: now can u get it to end soon? lol

mrmagoo7: i am only sorry i didnt know sooner

mrmagoo7: the end results are not up to me, if it were i would castrate em all myself with a dull rusty spoon

mrmagoo7: unfortunately all we can do is wait and see what happens

buttercup71190: how soon until they go to trial?

mrmagoo7:   i dont know, sometimes it can take up to 8 months

buttercup71190:   from what date? october 28, 2004 the initial arrests?

mrmagoo7:   well it can take up to 3 months for arraignment, and up to 8 months after that for actual court dates . . . .

mrmagoo7:   yes oct 28

mrmagoo7:   now . . . . they will probably have a couple court dates about a month apart to decide whether to plead guilty, try to work out a deal or decide to go to trial

mrmagoo7:   so you are looking at probably 1 to 1.5 years of actual court before its completely over . . . . and thats only for one court . . . .

mrmagoo7:   if they have to go to multiple courts it could take a few years . . . . depending on the extent of the charges, but . . . .

buttercup71190:   hopefully they plead guilty and get it over with

mrmagoo7:   the way they are pushing in the new laws, this could be a very good thing

mrmagoo7:   actually, i am hoping they dont plead and go to trial, only because the penalties will be much more

buttercup71190:   i just want them behind bars sooner

mrmagoo7:   i understand why you want it swift and over and i feel terrible for all that you have been thru

buttercup71190:   i dont like looking over my shoulder

mrmagoo7:   yes i know darlin, and it upsets me to no end

buttercup71190: with everything going on i dont know if it is my neighbor or them or my ex

mrmagoo7:   i know

buttercup71190: i hate not knowing

buttercup71190: then i dont know how to protect myself

mrmagoo7:   well i've been doing a pretty good job for ya

buttercup71190: i'm logging off

buttercup71190: Time, Event, Intruder, Count

5/1/2005 12:31:51 AM, TCP_Port_Scan, cm.coyotecableconnections.com, 29

buttercup71190: i'm starting to age quickly now with all the crap going on

buttercup71190: i just want a little peace

mrmagoo7:   well thats a shame, of all the people i've known in my life, you are probably the best person i have ever known . . . . you wouldnt hurt anyone for any reason, {barring the hackers of course} and even then i don't know . . . . but you are the most kind, most giving and most honest person, you truly have a big warm heart . . . . and i am honored to know you

mrmagoo7:   nah, you are not aging, more like a bottle of fine wine my dear

buttercup71190: lol

mrmagoo7:   anyway, go ahead and log off

June 6, 2005

buttercup71190: did u see the news?

mrmagoo7:   no i havent, anything good?

buttercup71190: yes the story, citi financial

mrmagoo7:   oh?

buttercup71190: yes hackers hacked pers info on ppl

mrmagoo7:   cool

buttercup71190: cant find the story online yet

mrmagoo7:   let me check my news feeds

buttercup71190: k i think this shocked citi financial. i think they had no clue until today

mrmagoo7:   really, what makes you think that darlin?

buttercup71190: check out their "privacy page" on their website

buttercup71190: they are soooooooooo secure

mrmagoo7:   what their link?

buttercup71190: not lol

buttercup71190: *http://www.citifinancial.com/* click on privacy

buttercup71190: i read something how they compared their security to bank of america who was hacked and how much better they were lol

mrmagoo7:   wow

mrmagoo7:   security is a thing of the past now with everything being computerized and tied together . . . . something has to change drastically soon

buttercup71190: did u find any articles?

mrmagoo7:   nope still looking

buttercup71190: that's another reason i think they didnt know what hit

mrmagoo7:   http://www.internetnews.com/storage/article.php/3510481

buttercup71190: usually the story is out on the net first

mrmagoo7: let me know if that loads for you

buttercup71190: it did

buttercup71190: there were also tapes that UPS lost too

mrmagoo7: 3.9 million

buttercup71190: the info was on the way to equifax

mrmagoo7: yep that would be the story, lol

buttercup71190: lol

buttercup71190: that was only a day not a week

mrmagoo7: well ya can never count on the media, lol

mrmagoo7: but there is gonna be more this week too, even aside from the law changes

mrmagoo7: there are a couple more stories supposed to surface this week in the news

buttercup71190: more? no way

mrmagoo7: according to the boards tonight yes way

buttercup71190: where is the hacking part of this story?

mrmagoo7: the tapes werent "lost," dont know why they said that . . . . but it will come out later this week i'm sure

buttercup71190: i was wondering about that

buttercup71190: maybe they havent caught them all yet

mrmagoo7: this was an inside job at the corporate office of citi financial

buttercup71190: wondering if its UPS employees or citi financial employees mrmagoo7:   lol

mrmagoo7:   you are way too cool ya know that!

buttercup71190:   so they were caught off guard

mrmagoo7:   i speaketh the truth, deal with it, lol

buttercup71190:   my gut is usually right

mrmagoo7:   http://www.antionline.com/showthread.
                     php?threadid=268536

mrmagoo7:   check that out

mrmagoo7:   just thought you should see that

buttercup71190:   what is this?

mrmagoo7:   its a message board as you know, but
                     there is a log file someone pasted in
                     there showing they were hacked . . . .
                     thought you might like to see the log
                     file just to see what it looked like

mrmagoo7:   http://www.wired.com/news/
                     technology/0,1282,67732,00.html

buttercup71190:   i wouldn't know what i was looking
                     at lol

mrmagoo7:   well that will change, thats why i
                     thought you might like to take a peek
                     at that

buttercup71190:   lol

mrmagoo7:   http://www.wired.com/news/
                     culture/0,1284,67709,00.html

buttercup71190:   Time, Event, Intruder, Count

                     6/6/2005 10:03:50 PM,
                     MSRPC_RemoteActivate_Bo,
                     S0106000ae62cf048.vc.shawcable.
                     net, 1

                     6/6/2005 9:58:01 PM, MSRPC_
                     RemoteActivate_Bo, ool-18b846a0.
                     dyn.optonline.net, 1

6/6/2005 9:53:49 PM,
MSRPC_RemoteActivate_Bo,
S0106000ae6999df6.vs.shawcable.
net, 1

6/6/2005 9:53:28 PM, MSRPC_
RemoteActivate_Bo, 1

6/6/2005 9:50:57 PM,
MSRPC_RemoteActivate_Bo,
S0106000244512f31.vc.shawcable.
net, 1

6/6/2005 9:50:01 PM,
MSRPC_RemoteActivate_Bo,
S01060010b5822a7d.ca.shawcable.
net, 1

mrmagoo7:   wonderful

buttercup71190: lol

buttercup71190: The list includes Impulse Marketing Group, WinSweepstakes, PrimeQ, Your Smart Rewards and MetaReward, which is owned by Experian, the credit report collector.

mrmagoo7:   so tell me something Angela . . . .

buttercup71190: what?

mrmagoo7:   is any of this starting to sink in yet: the ramifications of everything we did to get these guys has grown into something incredible

buttercup71190: starting to. it still seems surreal

buttercup71190: when you can't see the face behind the crimes being committed it is hard to comprehend

mrmagoo7:   yes but imagine all of these arrests and soon convictions of literally 10s of thousands of individuals, who might never been caught if we had not met

buttercup71190: thank brat

buttercup71190: although our paths almost crossed for years lol

mrmagoo7: i'm willing to bet i had run into you at some point . . . . but i think i would have definitely remembered you . . . . you are quite a lady

buttercup71190: now tell me something . . .

buttercup71190: how did citi financial come out of operation firewall?

mrmagoo7: because some certain people knew that those tapes were going to turn up missing, the information came out while investigating citi financials employees

mrmagoo7: remember that mail server i was in a few weeks back?

mrmagoo7: a lot of sensitive data came out of that session

buttercup71190: ohhhhhhhhhhhh i wont tell lol

mrmagoo7: ty, ya know thats it right there . . . . we trust each other and have right from the start

buttercup71190: y was everyone there under investigation? what tipped them off?

mrmagoo7: there was some corosponding emails between one of the employees and one of the ups drivers

mrmagoo7: oh all bank employees from every financial institution is under investigation right now because of all this cc stuff

buttercup71190: good its about time they know who works for them

buttercup71190: maybe now they will make it harder for just anyone to get those jobs

mrmagoo7:   i have to do a conference call

buttercup71190: k

mrmagoo7:   ty

mrmagoo7 has signed out. (6/6/2005 10:38 PM)

Chapter 10

The Alamo

August 6, 2005

mrmagoo7:   i didnt do it, lol

buttercup71190:   yahoo froze up on me

buttercup71190:   yes u did lol

mrmagoo7:   nu uh

buttercup71190:   ah ha

buttercup71190:   did u see who did that site?

buttercup71190:   jonathan

mrmagoo7:   no

buttercup71190:   look him up

mrmagoo7:   who is that?

mrmagoo7:   no i wont, lol

buttercup71190:   he's an attorney specializing in internet

mrmagoo7:   and you cant make me

buttercup71190:   then don't

buttercup71190:   i am hiring him

mrmagoo7:   to do what?

buttercup71190:   go after "Design-a-Site"

mrmagoo7:	bet he aint cheap
buttercup71190:	i am going to talk to him on tuesday
mrmagoo7:	how did you hear about him?
buttercup71190:	he came recommended through a friend
buttercup71190:	the same way i met u
buttercup71190:	ohhhhhhhhhhh maybe ur right. i might not want to meet him lol
mrmagoo7:	sa
buttercup71190:	he's been trying to get some laws changed about the internet
mrmagoo7:	he better stand in line, lol
buttercup71190:	he has written all sorts of topics
buttercup71190:	lol
buttercup71190:	told him i already did
mrmagoo7:	is he local?
buttercup71190:	long island
mrmagoo7:	oh he cant be all bad
mrmagoo7:	some of the brightest minds in this country come from there
buttercup71190:	lol or queens
mrmagoo7:	oh a jew, even better for a lawyer
buttercup71190:	he might have other motives to take the case
mrmagoo7:	such as?
buttercup71190:	to try to get some laws passed
buttercup71190:	Peter took my case for his own means too
mrmagoo7:	dunno, i was thinkin maybe he was a decendant of general custer
buttercup71190:	lol
buttercup71190:	not sure ask him
buttercup71190:	did u ask ur friends yet?
mrmagoo7:	dont even go there

buttercup71190: Y? what did they say?

mrmagoo7: i'm not talking about that subject anymore

buttercup71190: that bad?

mrmagoo7: so how bout them yankees huh?

buttercup71190: so did they say that i can tell u yet?

mrmagoo7: yes they did absolutely, lol

buttercup71190: lol no they didn't otherwise they would have told u themselves

buttercup71190: so what would I get if i told u?

mrmagoo7: a lighter sentence?

buttercup71190: lol

buttercup71190: what r u up to?

mrmagoo7: not much right now, you?

buttercup71190: just watching the news

mrmagoo7: anything good?

buttercup71190: no

buttercup71190: i was kind of hoping something's going to happen soon

mrmagoo7: i have no idea when it will happen

buttercup71190: how about never

buttercup71190: living like i do, everything feels like an eternity

mrmagoo7: what he hasnt been bothering you in a while now

mrmagoo7: the hackers are being taken care of

mrmagoo7: its not like everything is still the way it was

buttercup71190: i know

buttercup71190: just looking for closure

mrmagoo7: so am i, i hate this waiting game . . . . but at least something has been done about all these creeps buttercup71190:   i know

buttercup71190:   honestly when the nys internet crime division closed the case, i thought they all got away with it

mrmagoo7:   well i guess we showed them!

buttercup71190:   i would love to show that to the original investigator, Paul

mrmagoo7:   those guys should go back to arresting people for pulling tags off mattresses

buttercup71190:   lol

buttercup71190:   it would be fun to rub their faces in how close they were to a hugeeeeeeeeeeee case but quit.

buttercup71190:   imagine what their pensions would have been? lol

mrmagoo7:   pensions, just think of all the promotions and they probably would have become politictians, lol

buttercup71190:   lol

mrmagoo7:   listen, nobody ever would have thought that such a small investigation would have turned into what it did . . . . even the guys running the show cant believe they were able to expand this thing so big

buttercup71190:   i never did

buttercup71190:   at least they can see what's going on since i can't

mrmagoo7:   well they dont even get to see whats going on once the info is turned over

buttercup71190:   but they have more info on how everything is going down

buttercup71190:   and identities

buttercup71190: i have noticed a huge difference in the amount of spyware on sites. There's much less

mrmagoo7: yeah and spam is being attacked now, some new laws on that were just passed

buttercup71190: i also believe that google and other search engines are being forced to clean up their servers. a lot of dead sites are coming down

mrmagoo7: yeah so how can you say you cant see anything being done . . . . maybe not with a few people in particular . . . . but you are seeing alot of changes, and all because you didnt give up

buttercup71190: i just cant see who did what to me

buttercup71190: i want to see my attackers

mrmagoo7: well all that takes time, justice is very slow in this country

buttercup71190: i know

buttercup71190: did u see dateline tonight?

buttercup71190: ask ur friends who they know there lol

mrmagoo7: no

mrmagoo7: ?

buttercup71190: it was a story about a woman that was spammed with porn pics on her puter. the reporter investigated and traced it back to the person it came from.

mrmagoo7: oh??

buttercup71190: they showed how they hide behind the names of all the llc

buttercup71190: reminded me of "Design-a-Site" lol

mrmagoo7: yupper

buttercup71190: there was another story a few weeks ago

mrmagoo7: how do you think these guys make their money

buttercup71190: about the computer they found with the names of the terrorists. for some reason, nbc always has the stories first

buttercup71190: i wonder who they know lol

mrmagoo7: probably have some hired idiot breaking into servers and gettin the info, lol

buttercup71190: lol

buttercup71190: great minds think alike

buttercup71190: so when r u going to tell me everything?

mrmagoo7: everything about what?

buttercup71190: everything the idiot did to get the info

mrmagoo7: i dont understand?

buttercup71190: *mrmagoo7:* probably have some idiot breaking into servers and gettin the info, lol

mrmagoo7: ohhhhhhhhhhhhhhhhhhhhhhh, lol . . . . you dont miss a damned thing do ya, lol

buttercup71190: no i don't and i read between the lines

buttercup71190: the alamo knows lol

buttercup71190: u didnt find the answer on that website?

mrmagoo7: no, was i supposed to?

buttercup71190: maybe

mrmagoo7: i'm just gonna wait

buttercup71190:   u might even find it in this chat. u have to read between the lines

buttercup71190:   here's another hint

buttercup71190:   buttercup71190:   the alamo knows lol

mrmagoo7:   brb, my cheesecake should be done

mrmagoo7:   ib wondabar

mrmagoo7:   it bes a cheesecake

mrmagoo7:   now i have to refrigerate it til tomorrow

mrmagoo7:   you must be exhausted though, long week

buttercup71190:   i am

mrmagoo7:   you gonna be around tomorrow?

buttercup71190:   at one point yes

mrmagoo7:   what is that another riddle?

buttercup71190:   lol

mrmagoo7:   well why dont you get some rest and i'll talk to you tomorrow?

buttercup71190:   k

buttercup71190:   ttyt

mrmagoo7:   have a good night

buttercup71190:   u2

Chapter 11

The File

*N*ow that several months had passed since the original arrests of forty-eight people on October 28, 2004, identity theft became a household subject with crime after crime being exposed.

It was a beautiful summer evening when I decided to treat myself to a dinner. After changing my clothes into something more presentable, I hopped in my car and went to the restaurant that was located across the street from my house just a few doors down. It was always easier to take the car at night since, living in the country, the roads are not lit very well and there are no sidewalks to help protect one from oncoming cars.

The Heather's Haven Restaurant and Pub was an old Victorian that had been transformed into a restaurant. As the hostess escorted me to the back of the restaurant, I settled at a table that was situated overlooking the beautiful Catskill Mountains. Tonight I was craving their delicious chicken Francaise. The chef always prepared this dish perfectly. I ordered the chicken Francaise over linguine with the same sauce over the pasta. That was my favorite dish. Whenever I ate dinner there, I had to order their homemade Key lime pie for dessert. They had the best pie right up to and including the limes from the Keys. Just the thought of the taste of the lime would make my mouth water.

After paying for my dinner, I began to exit the restaurant. There were three dining areas that I had to go through before exiting. Upon reaching the bar area, I noticed that my personal attorney, Peter Columbo, was sitting at the bar. After leaving numerous phone messages and not receiving any calls back, I made my way to him where he was sitting with his girlfriend. After a few minutes of introductions, his girlfriend went to talk to someone else she knew. However, someone accidentally bumped into her.

Now I had a few minutes to ask him about what was going on with my case. He was handling a personal dispute for me. I wanted to know what the status of the case was. As I was speaking to him, there was a guy who was standing near the front door of the restaurant who caught my eye. Someone had approached him to speak with him. However, I noticed that he did not respond to him. After several attempts to engage him into a conversation, he persisted in his silence.

He stood at the end of the bar. He was tall with a rather large build and dark hair and was drinking a beer. As I watched him over my attorney's shoulder, I realized that he was one of my "protectors." He then looked up several times at me. He looked so familiar to me, but I could not place where I knew him from. The bar area was rather noisy since it was very busy for a summer Saturday evening. The next thing I knew was my attorney's girlfriend was engaged in a physical fight. All hell broke loose. The bartender quickly called the local police for backup. What started out to be a quick conversation suddenly turned chaotic. I told my attorney that I did not want to be there for when the police showed up. Since I had enough going on in my life, I decided to exit quickly. Following behind me, my attorney and his girlfriend also exited and were able to peel out of the driveway before I even made it to my car.

I arrived home a minute later relieved that I was not in the middle of the fight. A short while later James messaged me.

back::vindicator4u: "we were quite concerned with
Mr. Columbo's state of mind and

	his interaction with Ms. Hart tonight"
hackvindicated:	lol
hackvindicated:	what else?
hack::vindicator4u:	not funny
hack::vindicator4u:	they were quite upset
hackvindicated:	good
hackvindicated:	glad they saw
hack::vindicator4u:	good?
hackvindicated:	i am getting screwed by him
hack::vindicator4u:	yes good that it was witnessed, bad that it occurred
hackvindicated:	i didnt do anything wrong
hack::vindicator4u:	no you absolutly did nothing wrong
hackvindicated:	i just wanted to find out from him why he's not returning my calls and doing what i paid him to do
hack::vindicator4u:	"any further similar type actions may require increased security"
hackvindicated:	why?
hackvindicated:	what happened after i left?
hack::vindicator4u:	because they seem to think you told him about the WTP
hackvindicated:	no
hack::vindicator4u:	they believe Peter to be a "security risk"
hack::vindicator4u:	he could not have found out from any other source they say . . . .
hackvindicated:	i never said anything to him about it
hack::vindicator4u:	is it possible you mentioned being watched and he is just saying he knows to impress you?

hackvindicated:	he made a comment to me on a previous visit to his office and said something that led me to believe that he knew something
hackvindicated:	i never confirmed or denied anything
hackvindicated:	Peter is not involved in the "Design-a-Site" or computer case at all only my neighbor problem
hack::vindicator4u:	If Mr. Columbo becomes aware of the situation in his current state of mind, then Ms. Hart can no longer be protected in her present environment"
hack::vindicator4u:	i am trying to smooth this over
hackvindicated:	ok
hack::vindicator4u:	was anyone with you tonight and were you followed?
hackvindicated:	i am not sure if i was followed. i didnt see anyone
hack::vindicator4u:	they seem to believe you were not alone
hackvindicated:	i was not alone
hack::vindicator4u:	oh ok
hack::vindicator4u:	crap i told em that i thought you were
hackvindicated:	lol
hack::vindicator4u:	i have to close the room. i will straighten this out and call you in a little while,
hack::vindicator4u:	i was in error when i told you that she was alone . . . . she was with a friend . . . . i had not had a chance to talk to her but for a few minutes and was under

the impression that she was by herself

hack::vindicator4u: i do not want anyone making any moves on this until i straighten it out, understand me . . . . i am dead serious in this matter

hack::vindicator4u: "We will allow you to provide us with further information regarding this situation and re-evaluate the matter."

My phone rang. It was James.

"What the hell happened tonight?" he screamed.

"What are you talking about?" I inquired.

"I just got a frantic phone call from 'my friends.' They are ready to pick you up by helicopter and place you in the witness protection plan."

"What are you talking about? I am not in any danger that I know of. Or am I?"

"What happened? Tell me. They are coming to get you."

"I don't know what you are talking about. I just went out for dinner at Heather's Haven. On my way out, I stopped to talk to my attorney, who was sitting at the bar. I needed to find out what was going on in my personal matter. He does not know anything about the case. Only my mother and you know what is going on. So why would I be in any danger? They have arrested everyone in my case, right?"

"Your case has led to over four thousand investigations being started, some of whom are connected to your case directly, and over sixty-four thousand people have been arrested. What happened tonight that the police had to be called?"

"My attorney's girlfriend started a fight with someone. What would that have to do with me having to be picked up? As far as I know I am not in any danger."

"Well, one of your protectors . . ."

"You mean the one that was standing at the end of the bar? Tall, dark hair, big build . . . with a beer!"

"Yes, that's him. He thinks that you spoke to your attorney about him and exposed him."

"Well, no, I did not. However, even if I had, why should that result in my being picked up and put into the witness protection plan? I did not do anything wrong. He does not even know anything about my case, only that my identity had been stolen. I was discussing my personal litigation matter. It had nothing to do with the case. Besides, he made a few mistakes. If he thinks his identity was exposed, then they should take him off the case and put someone else on. I thought they were not supposed to follow me into a building. You told me that they need to stay within a 'watchful distance.' Not only that, but if he was working, then why was he drinking on the job?"

"All I know is that they are coming to pick you up shortly."

"Well, tell them that unless I know why they think I am in danger, then they are not going to pick me up and place me into any witness protection plan. I still don't know why they think I am in danger. If my 'protector' let me know who he was when he refused to speak to anyone in the restaurant, watching me move around the restaurant, and refused to say anything to me when someone pushed me into him, then he exposed himself, not me."

"This is serious. They are coming for you. This is not a game."

"I know it is *not* a game. Now tell me why I am in danger."

"Remember the other day, you came across an article on the internet about Able Danger."

"Yes, but what does that have to do with me?"

"That was the name of a file that was discovered on one of the hacker's computer, the same hacker who was in your computer."

"It was not on mine, right?"

"That's what I said."

"How would that put me in danger?"

"That is what I am trying to tell you." Then he paused for a moment and then continued, saying, "Do you remember when they changed the color of the money on the bills?"

"Yes . . ."

"This File . . . Let me start by saying that I had to use the Excel files that you gave me from your firewall logs. You had spent hours putting together those log files into Excel so that we could sort them by IP address. When I did, I mentioned to my 'Friends' that there were three IP addresses that stood out the most. My 'Friends' got a warrant, and I was able to get into the three machines. However, while in this one server, I noticed a file that was encrypted, and it was so big in size. So I retrieved it. After spending several days decrypting the 'File,' I finally saw what it was. You have no idea how big this is!"

"What was in the 'File'?"

"It contained copies of all of the original plates that they use to make identification or, in this case, false identifications for identity theft. It included copies of all fifty states' driver's licenses, Medicare cards, Medicaid cards, social security cards, passports, flight identifications, MasterCard, Visa, American Express and Discover cards, and badges for the FBI, CIA, USSEC, NASA, FISA, and DOJ."

"*Wow*! I had no idea! However, what does this have to do with them picking me up? Are we being set up? Why would I have to leave my friends and family because of this hacker or my 'protector' who feels his identity was exposed? I don't have a copy of this 'File,' nor did I know of the 'File' until now."

"I need to go now and make the phone call to them. I have an idea."

It seemed as though time were standing still. What seemed like an eternity was in reality only about half an hour before he called me back. He needed this time to implement his idea, whatever that was.

Then the call came, "It worked!" he screamed.

"What worked?" I inquired.

"They agreed not to pick you up by helicopter tonight," he said.

"What did you say to convince them not to pick me up?"

"I told them what you told me. First of all, if one of your protectors thought that his identity had been compromised, then they should remove him from the case and reassign someone. They agreed."

"I thought that my 'watchers' were only supposed to follow me from a distance and not follow me into a public place, such as the restaurant. Besides, what was the guy doing drinking on the job?"

"Well, reasoning with them worked. Just don't get into this situation again," he said, laughing.

"I can't believe you are laughing like this when my stomach is in knots! This is my life these people are trying to take me away from. I feel like I am fighting for my life. This is not fun!"

"Once again your intuition was right," he said.

"So much for your idea," I said with a nervous laugh. "I gave you everything to say."

"And it worked," he replied. "But they are going to be watching your attorney for the next three days."

"Well, let them. He knows nothing about the case. He was hired to handle a civil matter for me."

"They are going to. They will let us know if they change their minds."

"Even if they do, *I am not going anywhere*! And in case you don't know, *I mean it*!"

"I know."

"Right now, I need to go lie down. My stomach is in knots."

"Get some good sleep."

"Like that is going to happen. One good thing came out of this. Since the government has not handled my case by their law, I am under no obligation to them. That is really protecting me. There is *no* signed agreement with them. Now it is my option whether to tell the truth to the public or let them continue hiding their lies. I cannot help but feel that we are being set up. It's just a gut feeling. Why would someone want me out of the picture? I wonder what this has to do with the File."

At least I was out of danger for the moment. Being relocated, which meant being taken away from my friends and my family, did not make any sense to me. Was I really in danger? Perhaps my bodyguards were not all that smart. Their demeanor, dress, and actions usually gave them away. When someone is speaking to you in public, especially at a bar, people usually feel free to talk. After witnessing that a person is not speaking to anyone, except the bartender, that is usually a sign. If they thought that their identity had been compromised, instead of removing me from my life, they should replace him with someone else. My gut was telling me that somebody wanted me out of the picture, and somehow it was tied in to the File. By removing me from the picture, there would be no one else knowledgeable about the File except my computer guy. Then they would have to figure out what to do with him. The question remained, why?

Chapter 12

The Sting

S o much had happened in the two and a half years that had passed since the start of my case, Operation Firewall. We needed to connect the dots and quickly. The walls were closing in fast. There were some people who were working on our case that wanted us out of the picture.

You have received 1 file from mrmagoo7.

dojj.html.sda.exe

Open (Alt+Shift+O)

mrmagoo7:	i think i need a drink
hackvindicated:	hold on
mrmagoo7:	k
hackvindicated:	where is it
mrmagoo7:	dunno, i closed it
mrmagoo7:	its all over the place
hackvindicated:	k
mrmagoo7:	"find" in page "supreme"
hackvindicated:	can't read this
hackvindicated:	call me

mrmagoo7:	k
hackvindicated:	omg
mrmagoo7:	end of second line and beginning of 3rd
mrmagoo7:	http://www.usdoj.gov/jmd/ethics/
mrmagoo7:	http://a257.g.akamaitech.net/7/257/2422/11feb20051500/edocket.access.gpo.gov/cfr_2005/janqtr/5cfr2635.106.htm
mrmagoo7:	http://a257.g.akamaitech.net/7/257/2422/11feb20051500/edocket.access.gpo.gov/cfr_2005/janqtr/5cfr2635.107.htm
mrmagoo7:	http://www.access.gpo.gov/nara/cfr/waisidx_05/5cfr2635_05.html
mrmagoo7:	(c) A violation of this part or of supplemental agency regulations, as such, does not create any right or benefit, substantive or procedural, enforceable at law by any person against the United States, its agencies, its officers or employees, or any other person. Thus, for example, an individual who alleges that an employee has failed to adhere to laws and regulations that provide equal opportunity regardless of race, color, religion, sex, national origin, age, or handicap is required to follow applicable statutory and regulatory procedures, including those of the Equal Employment Opportunity Commission.
mrmagoo7:	if one of the guys in the group . . . .
mrmagoo7:	had me go into the server illegally . . . .

mrmagoo7: before a warrant was issued or some other technicality . . . . Ash's the oil off until i

mrmagoo7: i plead the fifth on everything

mrmagoo7: are they perceiving this as me accusing one of the guys

mrmagoo7: did something wrong, or protecting one of them

hackvindicated: i read and reread

mrmagoo7: figure anything out from all that mess?

hackvindicated: kind of but not sure

mrmagoo7: i think i need an attorney now

hackvindicated: not sure about that

mrmagoo7: wonder what they charge to go to the Supreme Court, lol

hackvindicated: it is not about you

mrmagoo7: think i'm screwed, lol

hackvindicated: someone's head is on the block now and it is not yours

hackvindicated: let me know when u can call

mrmagoo7: k, just give me a sec,

mrmagoo7: you on the phone?

hackvindicated: no

mrmagoo7: wanna bet

mrmagoo7: http://www.access.gpo.gov/nara/cfr/ waisidx_05/5cfr2635_05.html

mrmagoo7: (c) A violation of this part or of supplemental agency regulations, as such, does not create any right or benefit, substantive or procedural, enforceable at law by any person against the United States, its agencies, its officers or employees, or any other person. Thus, for example, an individual who alleges that an employee has failed to adhere (Be advised, you may be called to testify in US Supreme Court in Washington DC on or about 16/01/06 notification to follow) to laws and regulations that provide equal opportunity regardless of race, color, religion, sex, national origin, age, or handicap is required to follow applicable statutory and regulatory procedures, including those of the Equal Employment Opportunity Commission.[Code of Federal Regulations] [Title 5, Volume 3] [Revised as of January 1, 2005] From the U.S. Government Printing Office via GPO Access [CITE: 5CFR2635.106] [Page 551-552] TITLE 5—ADMINISTRATIVE PERSONNEL CHAPTER XVI—OFFICE OF GOVERNMENT ETHICS PART 2635_ STANDARDS OF ETHICAL CONDUCT FOR EMPLOYEES OF THE EXECUTIVE BRANCH—Table of Contents Subpart A_General Provisions Sec. 2635.106 Disciplinary and corrective action. (a) Except as provided in Sec. 2635.107, a violation of this part or of supplemental agency regulations may be

mrmagoo7:	whats up?
hackvindicated:	found another message
hackvindicated:	what does this mean
hackvindicated:	[CITE: 5CFR2635.106]
mrmagoo7:	probably just a duplicate of what they sent me
mrmagoo7:	forward it over

hackvindicated: i know the numbers are the section it is in

mrmagoo7: it looks like a key

hackvindicated: what is the rest

mrmagoo7: dunno

mrmagoo7: i would have to run it

hackvindicated: would it open the contract or did u already

mrmagoo7: no i havent been able to open it yet

mrmagoo7: the key is incomplete

hackvindicated: whats missing?

mrmagoo7: the key they sent me is incomplete

mrmagoo7: i need more, maybe that is the rest of it

hackvindicated: is this the other part

hackvindicated: lol

mrmagoo7: possibly

hackvindicated: or is it telling you how to respond in court?

hackvindicated: to cite some saying

mrmagoo7: wont know til i run it

hackvindicated: or maybe its part of the code of ethics

mrmagoo7: it could be the colonels secret recipe

hackvindicated: lol

mrmagoo7: who is it from?

hackvindicated: it was in their text on that email

hackvindicated: also notice where they warned u

hackvindicated: Thus, for example, an individual who alleges that an employee has failed to adhere (Be advised, you may be called to testify in US Supreme Court in Washington DC on or about 16/01/06 notification to follow) to laws and regulations that provide equal opportunity regardless of race, color, religion, sex, national origin, age, or handicap is required to follow applicable statutory and regulatory procedures, including those of the Equal Employment Opportunity Commission. [Code of Federal Regulations] [Title 5, Volume 3] [Revised as of January 1, 2005] From the U.S. Government Printing Office via GPO Access [CITE: 5CFR2635.106] [Page 551-552] TITLE 5—ADMINISTRATIVE PERSONNEL

hackvindicated: an individual who alleges that an employee has failed to adhere (Be advised, you may be called to testify in US Supreme Court in Washington DC on or about 16/01/06 notification to follow) to laws and

mrmagoo7: where did you get that?

hackvindicated: from that pic

hackvindicated: it is the exact text from it

mrmagoo7: ok, what does that have to do with the email you just got?

hackvindicated: didnt get an email

hackvindicated: the pic u sent

hackvindicated: that email

mrmagoo7: ohhhhhhhhhhhhhhhhh

mrmagoo7: i'm awake, lol

hackvindicated: lol

hackvindicated: do u understand anything i just said?

mrmagoo7: yes now i do

hackvindicated: they did not quote the whole law . . . only parts of it that applied to what they are being charged with

mrmagoo7: ok

He finally had received the last part of the key. When he accessed their message, the government of the United States had rewritten his contract. Once he made me aware of this change, it only made me feel that there was a mastermind behind this plot to remove us from this case. I still did not understand why they wanted us off the case. We had spent well over two years tracking, organizing, proving, and forwarding the information to the proper authorities.

Once again, he called me. Neither one of us could sleep. The anxiety of the case was starting to affect our health. We discussed the events of the past few months in detail. Sometimes hearing each other's thoughts helps to try to make sense of the situation. That was what was happening tonight.

"We really need to talk. We need to figure out who is behind this plot and why. Somehow, this has to be tied into the Alamo."

"You need to start talking. I need to know what the Alamo is."

"Do you know who Daniel Polk is?"

"Who?"

"I said Daniel Polk."

"Who?"

"Daniel Polk."

"Daniel Polk."

"That is what I said, Daniel Polk."

"How do you know him?"

"That is a long story. Who is he?"

"I can't believe you know who he is."

"I don't know who he is. Who is he?"

"He is the guy who is heading your case in the Department of Justice."

"You have to be kidding!"

"No, he is heading your computer investigation."

"Remember you gave me a message from your friends last July? They said, 'Remember the Alamo. This too shall pass.' Then I gave you a response to give them, 'I knew it, I knew it, I knew it!'"

"How could I forget? Neither you nor the guys would tell me what this meant. It was a running joke for months."

"During the previous winter, someone stayed at my bed-and-breakfast for the weekend. As I showed him to the room, we stopped in the living room for a short while. When I inquired about what brought him to the area, he said that he loves history. He especially loved the history about the Alamo. He proceeded to tell me about the battle at the Alamo. History was never my strong suit in school. In fact, that was my worst subject. The conversation was so bizarre. Unable to verbally respond, I stood there contemplating the purpose of this conversation. I remember looking at him and burning his image in my brain. He reminded me of a motorcycle-gang member. My first thought was that either he was one of the hackers or he was one of my protectors. Having a full house of people, I was not nervous about him staying. Feeling very uncomfortable about the conversation, I changed the subject. After showing him to his room, I retired to my room."

"If he was working on your case, he should not have been talking to you. How do you know who he is?"

"Here is where the story gets good. It was not until you gave me the message from your Friends in July to 'remember the Alamo, this too shall pass' when I realized who he was. When you gave me that message, it was then that I realized he was working on my case. This was almost half a year later. His conversation with me in my living room stood out in my head. I felt relieved to know that he was on the right side of the law or so I thought. Going back through my reservation book, I came across the name Mike F. McCusker, which I thought looked similar to another name, the general of the Alamo, Custer. I went to switchboard.com to look up his name. No results were found for the name. However, I did a reverse lookup by his phone number. It came back with the address he had given me but with a different name, Daniel Polk. I googled Daniel Polk's name. It brought me to about four different Web sites. It mentioned that he had a degree in mathematics and algorithms, knowledge that computer programmers need."

"Wow! You did your homework. Now I will tell you who he is. The night that they wanted to pick you up and place you in the witness protection plan, he was the one who made the phone call to me."

"You are kidding me! Now I have another question for you. Who wrote the original contract between you and the government to remain anonymous?"

"He did. You don't think . . . ?"

"I need you to look up in your e-mail and see who sent you the new contract in which you were no longer able to remain anonymous." There was a short pause.

"Son of a gun! He sent it to me. I don't understand all of this. He is the one who sent me the message on November 22, 2005, at 11:09 PM that said I may be called to testify in the U.S. Supreme Court., which said in part

> *"an individual who alleges that an employee has failed to adhere (Be advised, you may be called to testify in US Supreme Court in Washington DC on or about 16/01/06 notification to follow) to laws and"*

"Then on November 23, 2005, to 10:25 PM, a day later, he sent me the following message.

> *Hack:: Request for Security Clearence is denied. Suspension of privilages will continue until further notice. Room unavailable at this time. Protection order has been revolked. Please remain inside the U.S. until Order is lifted)*

"I received that e-mail right after they sent me the message that they were going to bring me up on charges. I definitely am being set up. Somehow he turned the whole situation around and got himself out of trouble, by putting me in the middle of it."

"Now that we have identified Daniel Polk as the person behind the scheme, we need to figure out why he would want us out of the picture. I am positive that this relates to the File. When was this File found on the hacker's server?"

"It was when your case started, sometime around July of 2003."

"When did the war start?"

"That was in February of 2003."

"That would mean the war started prior to the File being discovered."

"What does that have to do with your case?"

"Have you been watching the news lately? The media has been putting a lot of pressure on George Bush. They want to know why he went to war if he knew that the information that he was supposedly basing his decision on was faulty."

"I am lost."

"Let me finish. What if the president is trying to backdate the file and was trying to use it as the reason why he went to war. Perhaps then the media would back off from him. Since the File was found during my case, I would feel horrible if he would use it as the reason why he went to war and killed thousands of people. I do not want any of that bloodguilt on me or my God. My God is one of love, peace and justice. He views life as sacred."

"If you are right, then the orders originated from the top."

"Think about it. Valerie Plame's husband was about to go public with information that the president knew that his decision to go to war was based on faulty information. Shortly afterward, his wife's name, Valerie Plame, was leaked by the order of Dick Cheney. This was an excuse for the government to put them both into the witness protection plan. It seems to me that they were trying to prevent the information from becoming public knowledge. In other words, they were trying to protect *their* secrets. It sounds like what they are trying to do to us. If they are trying to backdate this File, they would need to make sure that neither one of us make the information public knowledge. You and I are the only ones who know that the File was found during Operation Firewall. Then it was code-named Able Danger."

"If you are right, then there is nothing that these people won't do for their commander in chief."

"I don't care who these people think they are. They are not going to remove me from my life, my friends, or my family. They are in for a fight. I was the one who was the victim, and you were the one who agreed to help me regain my identity.

We have done nothing wrong, but yet we are the ones being set up to take the fall. The witness protection plan was designed to protect the witness. However, in this case, they are trying to protect their secrets and could care less about our lives. I hate living having to always look over my shoulder. That is not living."

A few days later, on November 27, 2005, at 3:46 PM I received the following e-mail from the Department of Justice, with the following text.

> *HACK:: Please accept our sincere apology to you and Alamo for the events which unfolded in the previous weeks. The one responsible has been removed and transferred to an unknown location for further interrogation and will be prosecuted. Our thanks, <Kermit>*

The story around the text was as follows.

> A CIA report last October mentioned the allegations but did not give them full credence, stating, "we cannot confirm whether Iraq succeeded in acquiring uranium ore." Because of the doubts, Tenet said he never included the allegations in his own congressional testimonies or public statements about Iraqi efforts to obtain weapons of mass destruction. In a carefully scripted mea culpa, the White House on Friday blamed the CIA for its January misstep and Tenet finished the job hours later with a dramatic statement accepting responsibility.

> Bush's assertion in his State of the Union address in January that Iraq had sought nuclear materials from Africa "did not rise to the level of certainty which should be required for presidential speeches, and CIA should have ensured that it was removed," Tenet said. "It was a mistake," he added. *(HACK:: Please accept our sincere apology to you and Alamo for the*

events which unfolded in the previous weeks. The one responsible has been removed and transferred to an unknown location for further interrogation and will be prosecuted. Our thanks, <Kermit>) The one-two punch was designed to quell a growing political storm, fueled in part by members of Congress and Democratic presidential hopefuls, that challenged the credibility of the administration's arguments that Iraq was trying to reconstitute its nuclear weapons program before the U.S. invasion in March. Administration officials said that despite the miscue they did not expect Tenet to resign. He is the lone holdover from the Clinton administration and, while distrusted by some conservatives, has enjoyed Bush's confidence. "I've heard no discussion along those lines," CIA spokesman Mark Mansfield said Friday night when asked whether Tenet might consider resigning. National security adviser Condoleezza Rice, traveling with Bush in Africa, said Tenet still enjoyed the president's confidence.

The current controversy evolves around Bush's assertion in his State of the Union address that Iraq had tried to buy uranium from the African country of Niger. A month later, the administration retracted the allegation after learning that the British intelligence it was based upon had been forged. Tenet acknowledged Friday that the CIA had tried unsuccessfully for months to substantiate the British allegation and that State Department intelligence analysts believed the claim was "highly dubious," yet neither stopped Bush from making the claim in a single sentence of his annual address to the nation.

"These 16 words should never have been included in the text written for the president," Tenet conceded in a statement. "Let me be clear about several things right up front," he said. "First, CIA approved the president's State of the Union address before it was delivered. Second, I am responsible for the approval process in my agency. And third, the president had every reason to believe that the text presented to him was sound."

The director took his cue from Bush and Rice, who hours earlier blamed the error on the CIA. "I gave a speech to the nation that was cleared by the intelligence services," Bush told reporters in Uganda. If the CIA director had concerns about the information, "these doubts were not communicated to the president," Rice added. Key members of Congress called for someone to be held accountable. "The director of central intelligence is the principal adviser to the president on intelligence matters. He should have told the president. He failed. He failed to do so," said Senate Intelligence Committee chairman Pat Roberts, R-Kan. Tenet said there were "legitimate questions" about the CIA's conduct, and he sought in his statement to explain his agency's role. He said CIA officials reviewed portions of the draft speech and raised some concerns with national security aides at the White House that prompted changes in the language. But he said the CIA officials failed to stop the remark from being uttered despite the doubts about its validity. "Officials who were reviewing the draft remarks on uranium raised several concerns about the fragmentary nature of the intelligence with National Security Council colleagues," Tenet said. "Some of the language was changed. From what we know now, agency officials in the end concurred that the text in the speech was factually correct that the British government report said that Iraq sought uranium from Africa." CIA officials recognized at the beginning that the allegation was based on "fragmentary intelligence" gathered in late 2001 and early 2002, the director said. A former diplomat was sent by the CIA to the region to check on the allegations and reported back that one of the Nigerien officials he met "stated that he was unaware of any contract being signed between Niger and rogue states for the sale of uranium during his tenure in office," Tenet said. "The same former official also said that in June 1999 a businessman approached him and insisted that the former official meet with an Iraqi delegation to discuss 'expanding commercial relations' between Iraq and Niger. The former official interpreted the overture as an attempt to discuss uranium sales," Tenet said. The diplomat sent to the region has alleged he believed Vice President Dick Cheney's office was apprised of the findings of his trip. But Tenet said the CIA "did not brief it to the president, vice president or other senior administration officials." Tenet said that when British officials in fall 2002 discussed making the Niger information public, his agency expressed their reservations to the British about the quality of the intelligence.

Seeing this text around the message validated my previous assumptions.

Chapter 13

New Revelations

*T*he revelation about the File helped me to figure out the possible ramifications if such a file got out into the public. While conversing with my computer guy, he told me the File was worth one hundred forty million dollars ($140,000,000). He said that the File had been purchased on the black market for this amount. Realizing its value, now I understood how this file could attract all the wrong people. However, I had not even known about this file until August of 2005, a little over two years of the official start date of Operation Firewall. Not only did I have no previous knowledge of this file, I also had never even seen it. It was found on the server of one of the original hackers. Up until this point, it was never in my possession. This was the first time I was told about the file.

My curiosity got the best of me. At this time, I researched Able Danger. There were numerous ideas expressed on the Internet about what Able Danger was. However, no one knew what it really was. I believe the government was trying to prevent me from learning about the File. In other words, the government was trying to place me in their witness protection plan in order to prevent me and the public of learning about this File and keep their secret from becoming public knowledge. After all, the witness protection plan does not protect the person but protects the government's secrets. It was not until much later that I learned why.

All of his efforts did not stop them from having him testify at the CIA building in Virginia about the file. As promised, he came up for a visit. He invited a friend of his, the one who helped me make a ghost copy of my computer and reformat it, for dinner. While sitting on my front porch at the table, there was a military helicopter flying just on the other side of the street from me. They were letting him know that they meant business and they were watching his every move. I told him not to worry but to tell the truth. Then he would have nothing to worry about.

He was really concerned about his freedom and, even more so, his life. Whatever the panel decided was the truth, he would have to live with it. He was afraid that they would change their minds just like the government did to him on several occasions. They had revised their contract with him. I guess when you have the power to do whatever you want and don't have to answer to anyone else, then you can get away with everything. He decided to make alternate arrangements that would be executed only if he was incarcerated. He gave me an encrypted CD. He gave his friend the key to decrypt it. We were given instructions to give the CD and the key to a few people. This was his insurance policy or his get-out-of-jail free card. Hopefully, we would not have to do this.

A few days later, he returned home to Virginia. On the day of his testimony, he was escorted to the airport. Boarding a helicopter, he was transported to the CIA building in Langley, Virginia. He proceeded to testify about the File. What only took several hours seemed like an eternity. The waiting was like watching paint dry.

After hearing his voice on the phone from the helicopter, I began to relax. Unfortunately, he was right. Like he had said earlier, they accused him of protecting the wrong people. Partway through his testimony, they slapped the handcuffs on him to try to intimidate him into testifying who he was covering for. He said that he thought they were going to lock him up. After having told him that my prayers were with him, I was elated that he was released from his captors. He said that he had been under so much stress and had not eaten or slept in days. He was glad it was over.

All things seemed to be quiet for a while. In the meantime, I had a phone conversation with my computer guy about writing a book about our escapades. We discussed characters' names that we would use in place of their real names. The story was going to be fictional but based on the real events. We received permission to do so.

The next day, I received an e-mail that looked like spam. Upon further inspection, the subject line included two of the characters' names that we had discussed on the phone the previous night when we were considering character names for the book. The text in the e-mail was all in military lingo. I forwarded the e-mail to my computer guy to scan. He had the government's program that they use to scan e-mails in order to pull out the seal with its message that was embedded as Word Art and not visible to the human eye. He pulled the seal out and forwarded a copy to me via instant message upload.

It was November 23, 2005, at 8:20 PM when I received the first message.

> *"(Hack:: Request for Security Clearance is denied. Suspension of privilages will continue until further notice. Room unavailable at this time. Protection order has been revolked. Please remain inside the U.S. until Order is lifted)"*

This sounded like he was in trouble. When the second message came in at 9:17 PM, it said,

> *"xxxxxAny attempt to leave the United States will result in imediate apprehension xxxxx"*

Yet another correspondence in the form of an e-mail again arrived from them at 10:20 PM. This time they included the following threat,

"(Hack:: The withholding of evidence pertaining to the illegal possession of government property can and will cost more than the price of ones freedom)."

There was no other way to interpret this sentence. The only cost that was more than the price of one's freedom would be death! This time they sent him a partial key to unlock the encrypted file that they had sent him the week before his testimony. Hopefully, this would unlock the contract and the government's agenda. The conversation below was the text that surrounded this message.

> *hackvindicated* (11/24/2005 12:01 AM): The government said Monday it plans to review his request for compensation, but said this would not affect the severe charges he faces.

> *hackvindicated* (11/24/2005 12:03 AM): Neither did Brin when Battelle asked him earlier this year about the potential perils of Google becoming a secret tool for the U.S. government.

> *hackvindicated* (11/24/2005 12:04 AM): Reviews are ordered only when there is a complaint.

> *hackvindicated* (11/24/2005 12:05 AM): We can assist.

> *hackvindicated* (11/24/2005 12:07 AM): Still, some called the document a breakthrough after so much debate, especially because many had started the day pessimistic that they would have an agreement at all.

> *hackvindicated* (11/24/2005 12:08 AM): Everyone's nervous, once you hand over your weapons you're exposed,"

> *hackvindicated* (11/24/2005 12:10 AM): The compromise document came after weeks of debate climaxed with several days of marathon negotiation.

hackvindicated (11/24/2005 12:16 AM): She appeared on the ABC morning show the day before a new MTV documentary chronicling her trip to a village in Kenya with U.N. adviser and economist

mrmagoo7 (11/24/2005 12:20 AM): give me about ten minutes ok

mrmagoo7 (11/24/2005 12:21 AM): i promise i will call you back

hackvindicated (11/24/2005 12:21 AM): k

mrmagoo7 (11/24/2005 12:37 AM): find anything?

hackvindicated (11/24/2005 12:37 AM): wanted to ask something

mrmagoo7 (11/24/2005 12:37 AM): yes?

hackvindicated (11/24/2005 12:37 AM): did u talk to a reporter at all?

mrmagoo7 (11/24/2005 12:37 AM): no never

mrmagoo7 (11/24/2005 12:38 AM): why?

hackvindicated (11/24/2005 12:38 AM): alot of text about talking to a reporter and they are subject to

hackvindicated (11/24/2005 12:38 AM): (Hack:: The withholding of evidence pertaining to the illegal possession of government property can and will cost more than the price of ones freedom)

mrmagoo7 (11/24/2005 12:38 AM): what the hell is that supposed to mean?

hackvindicated (11/24/2005 12:39 AM): they think u have the file

mrmagoo7 (11/24/2005 12:39 AM): what evidence?

mrmagoo7 (11/24/2005 12:39 AM): i'm a dead man

hackvindicated (11/24/2005 12:39 AM): no

hackvindicated (11/24/2005 12:39 AM): look at the ditto mark

mrmagoo7   (11/24/2005 12:39 AM): ditto mark?

hackvindicated (11/24/2005 12:39 AM): and i dont have anything

hackvindicated (11/24/2005 12:39 AM): Hack::

mrmagoo7   (11/24/2005 12:40 AM): no that partial file is nothing to them

mrmagoo7   (11/24/2005 12:40 AM): they want the whole one

mrmagoo7   (11/24/2005 12:40:AM): that partial file is just barely enough to prove something but not what . . . .

mrmagoo7   (11/24/2005 12:41 AM): the whole one is what they want

mrmagoo7   (11/24/2005 12:41 AM): is that what all of this is about? the (bleeping) File

hackvindicated (11/24/2005 12:41 AM): i think so. i think they think u have a copy

mrmagoo7   (11/24/2005 12:42 AM): i really dont look good in stripes ya know or jumpsuits

hackvindicated (11/24/2005 12:42 AM): stop

mrmagoo7   (11/24/2005 12:43 AM): if they just wanted the file they would have come to my door and asked for it

hackvindicated (11/24/2005 12:43 AM): no i dont think so

mrmagoo7   (11/24/2005 12:43 AM): its got to be more than that

mrmagoo7   (11/24/2005 12:43 AM): they want to use that against me

hackvindicated (11/24/2005 12:43 AM): withholding of evidence pertaining to the illegal possession of government property

mrmagoo7 (11/24/2005 12:44 AM): and what lawyer wrote that line?

hackvindicated (11/24/2005 12:44 AM): i know

mrmagoo7 (11/24/2005 12:44 AM): that looks like a charge, not a heads up

mrmagoo7 (11/24/2005 12:45 AM): i am in serious trouble here darling

hackvindicated (11/24/2005 12:45 AM): u didnt do anything

mrmagoo7 (11/24/2005 12:45 AM): if anyone asks, you dont know me, lol

hackvindicated (11/24/2005 12:45 AM): lol

mrmagoo7 (11/24/2005 12:46 AM): wonder if they are gonna make me hold the popcorn when they flip the switch on the chair, lol

hackvindicated (11/24/2005 12:46 AM): stop

mrmagoo7 (11/24/2005 12:46 AM): sorry

mrmagoo7 (11/24/2005 12:47 AM): this has got to be bullshit

mrmagoo7 (11/24/2005 12:47 AM): they cant do this to me for doing what they asked of me

mrmagoo7 (11/24/2005 12:47 AM): maybe they think i was holding back because i asked for a contract?

mrmagoo7 (11/24/2005 12:48 AM): ya know if they wanted me out of the group all they had to do was ask, lol

mrmagoo7 (11/24/2005 12:48 AM): now they have me second guessing everything i did and the way i did it

hackvindicated (11/24/2005 12:48 AM): no dont 2nd guess

hackvindicated (11/24/2005 12:49 AM): btw . .

hackvindicated (11/24/2005 12:49 AM): does hack refer to u or me?

mrmagoo7 (11/24/2005 12:49 AM): me, its my nic

hackvindicated (11/24/2005 12:49 AM): and mine?

mrmagoo7 (11/24/2005 12:49 AM): i added the vindicator part

hackvindicated (11/24/2005 12:50 AM): they know i am reading the messages they are sending u

mrmagoo7 (11/24/2005 12:50 AM): all of my messages are directed to hack

mrmagoo7 (11/24/2005 12:50 AM): no they dont

mrmagoo7 (11/24/2005 12:51 AM): that is how i am known in circles

mrmagoo7 (11/24/2005 12:51 AM): Hack::

mrmagoo7 (11/24/2005 12:52 AM): started as a typo years ago and i kept it

hackvindicated (11/24/2005 12:52 AM): k

mrmagoo7 (11/24/2005 12:53 AM): i'm sure they will give me a new nickname, like bitch lol

hackvindicated (11/24/2005 12:53 AM): stop

mrmagoo7 (11/24/2005 12:53 AM): brb, then i'll call

hackvindicated (11/24/2005 1:03 AM): k

hackvindicated (11/24/2005 1:03 AM): Reviews are ordered only when there is a complaint.

hackvindicated (11/24/2005 1:04 AM): who do u think?

mrmagoo7 (11/24/2005 1:04 AM): somebody very high up

hackvindicated (11/24/2005 1:04 AM): who might know about the ___ mrmagoo7   (11/24/2005 1:05 AM): like cheneys assistant or someone higher

mrmagoo7   (11/24/2005 1:05 AM): this has to go right to the top

mrmagoo7   (11/24/2005 1:06 AM): http://caselaw.lp.findlaw.com/data2/circs/dc/043138b.pdf

mrmagoo7   (11/24/2005 1:08 AM): http://news.findlaw.com/legalnews/lit/iraq/documents.html

mrmagoo7   (11/24/2005 1:25 AM): i found the file on the second machine

mrmagoo7   (11/24/2005 1:25 AM): all i had was an IP

mrmagoo7   (11/24/2005 1:25 AM): ok, now when they ask . . . .

mrmagoo7   (11/24/2005 1:26 AM): where did you get this file . . . .

mrmagoo7   (11/24/2005 1:26 AM): my anser i dont know . . . .

mrmagoo7   (11/24/2005 1:26 AM): i am covering up for a terrorist

backvindicated (11/24/2005 1:26 AM): u could say that u found the evidence by accident when you were looking for a different file

backvindicated (11/24/2005 1:27 AM): u had no idea whose machine it was

mrmagoo7   (11/24/2005 1:27 AM): only one problem with that . . . .

mrmagoo7   (11/24/2005 1:27 AM): the government has disavowed any knowledge of me in no uncertain terms . . . .

mrmagoo7   (11/24/2005 1:27 AM): i have no one at the agency to back me up mrmagoo7   (11/24/2005 1:28 AM): as far as anyone is concerned i did it all on my own . . . .

mrmagoo7   (11/24/2005 1:29 AM): and thats why the bastards had me plead the fifth, so they could not be implicated

backvindicated (11/24/2005 1:29 AM): now tell all

mrmagoo7   (11/24/2005 1:29 AM): in other words darling, i have been set up!

backvindicated (11/24/2005 1:29 AM): i thought u said u could trust them?

mrmagoo7   (11/24/2005 1:29 AM): tell what, whod believe me

backvindicated (11/24/2005 1:30 AM): i can talk

backvindicated (11/24/2005 1:30 AM): there is one that i can get in trouble

backvindicated (11/24/2005 1:30 AM): oh yes i do

backvindicated (11/24/2005 1:30 AM): the one who stayed at my house

backvindicated (11/24/2005 1:30 AM): not her

backvindicated (11/24/2005 1:30 AM): mike mccusker

backvindicated (11/24/2005 1:31 AM): aka

backvindicated (11/24/2005 1:31 AM): the name i told u on the phone

backvindicated (11/24/2005 1:31 AM): why? why? why?

backvindicated (11/24/2005 1:31 AM): polk

mrmagoo7   (11/24/2005 1:40 AM): http://news.findlaw.com/legalnews/lit/iraq/documents.html

mrmagoo7   (11/24/2005 1:41 AM): they used my file to go to war with iraq

mrmagoo7   (11/24/2005 1:41 AM): it was the excuse they used mrmagoo7   (11/24/2005 1:43 AM): i am gonna walk into court in dc and be charged as a terrorist

backvindicated (11/24/2005 1:43 AM): i wont let that happen. i will do everything i can to stop that

mrmagoo7   (11/24/2005 1:43 AM): i cannot let you do that

backvindicated (11/24/2005 1:44 AM): u arent asking

backvindicated (11/24/2005 1:44 AM): im offering and will

mrmagoo7   (11/24/2005 1:44 AM): you have done enough already

backvindicated (11/24/2005 1:44 AM): oh stop after all u did putting your neck on the line?

mrmagoo7   (11/24/2005 1:44 AM): and i dont want you implicated in something that is way over both our heads

backvindicated (11/24/2005 1:44 AM): at this point i really dont give a damn

mrmagoo7   (11/24/2005 1:45 AM): darlin, i would do it all again anyway . . . .

backvindicated (11/24/2005 1:45 AM): thats not the point

mrmagoo7   (11/24/2005 1:54 AM): what if i give them my full copy if they are willing to drop this

backvindicated (11/24/2005 1:55 AM): u can always make a dup

backvindicated (11/24/2005 1:55 AM): on a machine that is not on the net

backvindicated (11/24/2005 1:55 AM): thats what i was talking about

mrmagoo7   (11/24/2005 1:56 AM): no more dups, not this time mrmagoo7　　(11/24/2005 1:56 AM): should they pick me up they could drug me and find out the truth

hackvindicated (11/24/2005 1:56 AM): k

mrmagoo7　　(11/24/2005 2:08 AM): k, calling

hackvindicated (11/24/2005 2:08 AM): k

hackvindicated (11/24/2005 2:18 AM): He added it would be improper to rely on a German judge, unelected by the American people, since "he's playing a role in helping shape policy binding this nation.

mrmagoo7　　(11/24/2005 2:18 AM): henderson

hackvindicated (11/24/2005 2:20 AM): The compromise document came after weeks of debate climaxed with several days of marathon negotiation.

mrmagoo7　　(11/24/2005 2:21 AM): Angela, I am sorry i got you involved in all of this, please forgive me

hackvindicated (11/24/2005 2:21 AM): its not ur fault

hackvindicated (11/24/2005 2:21 AM): go blame Mandel lol

mrmagoo7　　(11/24/2005 2:22 AM): i should have kept all of this a secret from the very start and just let you think i was another scumbag who deserted you

hackvindicated (11/24/2005 2:22 AM): But he acknowledged that upholding past cases ensured "predictability, stability and legitimacy."

hackvindicated (11/24/2005 2:22 AM): Think "Freedom."

hackvindicated (11/24/2005 2:25 AM): dont do anything stupid please *backvindicated* (11/24/2005 2:25 AM): u got through the first segment

mrmagoo7　(11/24/2005 2:25 AM): i am gonna call their bluff

backvindicated (11/24/2005 2:26 AM): what is that?

mrmagoo7　(11/24/2005 2:26 AM): i am sending a message to the head of the doj

backvindicated (11/24/2005 2:26 AM): what message?

mrmagoo7　(11/24/2005 2:26 AM): i am gonna probably disappear after that

backvindicated (11/24/2005 2:27 AM): temp or perm?

mrmagoo7　(11/24/2005 2:27 AM): cause they will pick me up for sure

mrmagoo7　(11/24/2005 2:27 AM): i have put you thru too much and i want it to stop here and now

mrmagoo7　(11/24/2005 2:27 AM): i am sorry

backvindicated (11/24/2005 2:28 AM): its not your fault stop apologizing i wont accept it

mrmagoo7　(11/24/2005 2:29 AM): my phone is tapped

mrmagoo7　(11/24/2005 2:29 AM): i cant talk

mrmagoo7　(11/24/2005 2:29 AM): i dont want you any more hurt than you are

mrmagoo7　(11/24/2005 2:29 AM): i am sorry

mrmagoo7　(11/24/2005 2:30 AM): really sorry

mrmagoo7　(11/24/2005 2:30 AM): i just want to talk to them face to face so that i can end this shit

backvindicated (11/24/2005 2:31 AM): so what message are u going to send?

mrmagoo7　(11/24/2005 2:31 AM): you need your life back damn it *hackvindicated* (11/24/2005 2:31 AM): i want a copy of the original agreement

mrmagoo7   (11/24/2005 2:31 AM): and i am gonna give it to you

hackvindicated (11/24/2005 2:31 AM): this too shall end

mrmagoo7   (11/24/2005 2:31 AM): i will turn myself in and plead guilty to whatever they want

hackvindicated (11/24/2005 2:31 AM): noooooooooooooooooooooooooooo

hackvindicated (11/24/2005 2:32 AM): dont plead guilty to anything just turn the File over

hackvindicated (11/24/2005 2:38 AM): we can get through this

mrmagoo7   (11/24/2005 2:41 AM): if i get out of this alive,

mrmagoo7   (11/24/2005 2:48 AM): that i will turn over the file . . . .

mrmagoo7   (11/24/2005 2:49 AM): and under the condition that i will if called go to court and name names, places and events . . . .

mrmagoo7   (11/24/2005 2:50 AM): that along with the fact that they will know you will haunt them forever

hackvindicated (11/24/2005 2:50 AM): maybe use the fact that i know who one of them is and the alamo

mrmagoo7   (11/24/2005 2:51 AM): ok

mrmagoo7   (11/24/2005 2:51 AM): let me type this up

His heart began to pound. Immediately, he phoned me. He had just received another message that told him he needed to testify about the File. During the conversation, he mentioned that he could testify about the File and where it was found, but he could not say that it was found during Operation Firewall since the case was classified. He would have to plead the fifth to avoid giving that testimony. This sounded like a set-up to me. By not being able to testify that the file was found during Operation Firewall, it might sound as if he were protecting the wrong people. He then informed me that this File was owned by the United Nations who had purchased it illegally on the black market for $140,000,000. The File contained copies of all the original plates that the United States uses to make every form of identification. Passports; all drivers licenses for each state; Medicaid cards; Medicare cards; credit cards including MasterCard, Visa, American Express and Discover; United States currency; badges for the FBI, CIA, DOJ, and USSEC; flight licenses; and social security cards could be fraudulently made to look like the originals since they were generated from copies of the original plates.

Why would the United Nations have in their possession a file that contained copies of the original plates to make false identification? Why would they spend so much money in order to own such a file that is the property of the United States? Why would the government be so upset if my computer guy had a copy of this file when they should be upset that the United Nations had purchased this copy on the black market for $140,000,000? What purpose could this file have really been used for?

He then called me.

"You did not do anything wrong. When you found the file, didn't you turn it over to the government?"

"Yes. Remember the log files that you were keeping from your firewall? There were three IP addresses that stood out. Upon further investigation on the server of one of those IP addresses, there was a rather large file that was encrypted. I retrieved a copy of the File and spent days decrypting the file. I could not believe my eyes when I saw what it contained."

"Based on what you just said, that File was found on the hacker's server. What did you do next?"

"I turned it over to the government once I came to an agreement with them. Due to the content and value of the File, they had agreed that I could remain anonymous for my protection. I have a signed contract with them."

"Just remember who you are dealing with. They are known for not telling the truth. Now that you told me this, I know we are being set up. I just need to figure out who is behind it and why."

"I am really upset about having to testify. They told me I could remain anonymous. Now they changed their mind."

"You have not done anything wrong. You happened to find the File on the hacker's server. You turned it over to them. I am sure this is very unsettling, but you need to testify."

"I don't think I can do that. Right now my stomach is so upset that I feel sick."

"When do you have to testify?"

"In a few weeks."

"Well, if you have done nothing wrong, then you have nothing to worry about. Everything will work out."

"I don't think that you understand. If I testify about the file but plead the fifth on anything related to Operation Firewall, then it looks like I am protecting a terrorist."

"If you tell the whole truth and nothing but the truth, then you have nothing to fear. Why do you think they have changed their mind now?"

"I don't know, and I don't like it!"

"The last e-mail said, *"(Hack:: The withholding of evidence pertaining to the illegal possession of government property can and will cost more than the price of ones freedom)."*

"I told you they mean business."

"This sounds like a threat to your freedom. It sounds like they want to lock you up. Why would they want to do this? You have done nothing but help them track these guys and catch them. By any chance, do you still have a copy of the file?"

"I did keep one copy."

"I believe that they want you to turn over the copy of the File that you have."

"Do you think that is why they are doing this?"

"If you read their words carefully, they say 'the illegal possession of government property can and will cost more than the price of one's freedom.' Their choice of words, 'cost more than the price of one's freedom,' makes it sound like you will lose your life. If that is that case, they need to execute those in the United Nations who were involved in the illegal purchase of this file. I do not like this threat! This only proves my gut is right. We are being set up."

"I need to get away from this. Can I come up next weekend and review all of the details?"

"First things first. You need to turn over the copy of the file."

"I am going to send them an e-mail and set up a meet point."

"I'll let you go take care of business."

He sent them an e-mail of requesting a meet point.

> mrmagoo7 (11/24/2005 3:05:31 AM): to whom it may concern, this is to inform you that i am willing and ready to establish communication of encrypted data to your office via a go between . . . . on friday . . . . this will end our relationship and the need for any and all further services on your part . . . . should this not satisfy you, i will go public with my information . . . . i will consider this matter closed, and will not appear in court . . . . should this be unsatisfactory then i will expect an immediate reply please respond to alamo@ hackvindicated.com I will consider this matter closed as of friday 26/11/05. advise of anything further. please setup a meet point.

A short while later at 3:17 AM on November 24, 2005, they sent in their response, which was *"hack:: security clearance deniedaccepted meet point to follow goodbye."* This response was sent in by the Department of Justice's logo seal that was embedded in an e-mail. This was the first one that I received in color; otherwise, they were normally in black and white. I was told that the color meant they were happy.

My computer guy followed through with his promise. He delivered the copy of the file that he had kept in his possession to them. He arranged for another meet point to deliver the key to decrypt the CD at a later date. The United States government now had possession of their file.

Arrangements were made to pick up the key. Due to the content and value of the file, the key could not be delivered with the file. A separate drop was made for the key. However, someone who was working for the United Nations intercepted the drop. Now the United Nations had leverage against the United States so that they would not press any charges against them. Although the United Nations had no right to purchase this file on the black market for $140,000,000, they wanted to evade prosecution. Not only was the United States not allowed to press any charges against the United Nations, the United Nations also demanded money from the United States in exchange for the key to open the decrypted file that the United States already had in its possession.

Chapter 14

Judgment Day

HACK:: Please accept our sincere apology to you and Alamo for the events which unfolded in the previous weeks. The one responsible has been removed and transferred to an unknown location for further interrogation and will be prosecuted. Our thanks, <Kermit>

$\mathcal{T}$his message had come on November 27, 2005, at 3:46 PM. It was so hard for me to comprehend what had just happened. Our suspicions were right. Evidently, the night of my phone conversation with my computer guy yielded many helpful hints. Within the e-mail message sent, there were links to Web sites where Daniel Polk had posted information about the File, trying to backdate the File the night before. To see my suspicions in print blew my mind. These postings were made the day before the Revelations of my phone call. Subsequently we received notification that he and three others had been arrested in the plot. They all were transferred to an unknown location for further interrogation.

This led me to conclude that they were being transferred to the terror camps that were headlines in the news. Two of the four people arrested worked for the CIA and the other two for the Department of Justice. Feeling a sense of peace, I still did not allow myself to let down my guard. With these ones removed from my case, I felt more at ease. However, at the same time I felt unsettled. If I was right about Daniel Polk setting us up, was I also right about the reason why? Being right would mean that this went right up to the vice president and president of the United States. That would mean this was still not over. At least I was over another hurdle.

On Thursday, December 1, 2005, I received an e-mail that told me to watch over my shoulder at work on Friday, December 2. I did not know what to expect, only that something might happen.

One of my duties at work was to go to the bank. Around noontime, I departed toward the bank. As I pulled out of the driveway onto the highway, a truck pulled out in front of me. Across the back, *Phoenix* was written. This was a term that was being used in numerous e-mails with military lingo. Many state workers were out that day doing roadwork. The e-mail had referenced the hustle and bustle of the town and townspeople. It was as if the e-mails were being acted out.

Upon entering the bank, there was a man exiting who was carefully watching my every move. Believing that he was one of my protectors gave me a sense of security. After finishing my banking transactions, I exited the building. As I headed toward my car, another man was entering the bank and also was watching my every move. He also seemed to be talking to himself, or was he?

As I exited the driveway, I took a right-hand turn heading back towards work. On the left side of the road, I noticed two men talking. The guy facing me looked Greek. The guy who had his back toward me was wearing a trench coat. He stood with his hands in both his pockets. As I started to pass by them, this distinguished, well-kempt gray-haired man turned and made eye contact with me as I drove by them. Upon seeing his face, I screamed, "Oh my God!"

This was the insurance man who had been showing up at my house in the previous weeks. On each of the four occasions, I had company. My computer guy and his wife were there at least on one of the occasions. My mother happened to be at my house on the other occasions. The first time that my mother was there, I told him that I was not interested in the insurance. Each subsequent time, my mother told him that I was not interested in taking out the insurance. She said that on the occasion when I was sick, he did not believe her and tried to force his way into the house. I came out in my pajamas and told him to leave. I told him that I would be filing a complaint with the life insurance company. He had given me a name, which I can assume was not his real name. The following day, I had phoned the insurance company and explained what had happened. They confirmed that they did have a guy who worked for them by that name. However, when I described what he looked like, they told me it was not him. I asked them to take me off their visiting renewal list and send me everything through the mail. They agreed to do that for me.

Every time that this guy had stopped in to try to sell me the insurance, my gut would be in knots. For some reason, I believed that he did not work for the insurance company. After being reassured by them that their guy had not shown up at my house, I felt like my intuition was right.

When I had returned to work that Friday, I began to interpret the events of my trip to the bank. I could not comprehend why so many people were swarming around me. Needing to talk out my feelings, I phoned my mother. Anytime something bizarre happened around me, after speaking about it over the telephone, they usually were able to better protect me knowing what I had just experienced. After I had learned about the File, I could only conclude that there were many other agencies involved in the investigation. Some were there to help me, yet there were others who were there for their own means. There were those who were interested in protecting me, and there were those who were interested in protecting the terrorist. All I knew was that by discussing the events over the phone, at least the right agency would know what I just experienced.

Suggesting to my mother to go out to breakfast with me the following day on Saturday, December 3, 2005, I wanted her to see and hear what was going on. She needed to see how many people were swarming around me. She agreed to go to a local diner, Michael's Diner.

We entered the restaurant through the side door. Only the waitress and the cook were there. We seated ourselves at the booth to the right of the door. We placed our breakfast order. I told her to watch carefully because the place was about to fill up. A few minutes later two guys that looked Arabian walked in. Being that all the tables except ours were open, they seated themselves at the booth right behind my mother. They proceeded to have a conversation about the hustle and bustle of the area and mentioned a few things that were only mentioned in e-mails. The United Arab Emirates was a common theme in the e-mails. I also told her to watch for this younger blond haired guy who follows me around town. Also, there would be a guy with dark hair and a goatee. He usually followed me around at work and public events. He lived right up the road from me. Not only did both of them enter, but someone else that I did not expect. It was the guy who was standing on the side of the road, talking to the agent who had posed as an insurance inspector. A man and two women came in through the backdoor and walked past my table. While alongside my table, one of the women turned toward me and said, "Hello, Angela." My mother asked me if I knew who she was. I told her that I did not, but evidently she knew who I was by my first name.

All this happened before we were served our breakfast. While we were eating breakfast, another man came in and sat down on the bar stools at the counter next to the man whom I had first seen talking to the agent on the side of the road. They started having a conversation about my computer guy, even mentioning his name. My mother was shocked at all of the events.

She said, "I think you are really being protected."

I replied, "I feel like I am amongst a den of wolves."

"I prayed for three specific signs. Two of them have already come true. However, I am still waiting to see if the third thing comes true. All three signs need to come true in order for me to know this is the truth."

The third sign that she had prayed for never did come true. By the time we were ready to leave the restaurant, there were about twenty-five people there. Once finished, we drove back to my house. I told my mother that I needed to discuss the events that had just unfolded over the phone. Once again, I needed those monitoring my phones to know everything that had happened.

After dropping me off, she drove home to her house. As promised, she called me and we discussed the events. It was as if these people were telling me to trust in what I was reading in the e-mails.

*   *   *

Shortly after, I received an e-mail that told me they were going to pick me up. They told me to meet them at the local pharmacy. A helicopter would be sent to pick me up. Not knowing whether I could trust anything that they were telling me or who had sent me the e-mail, I packed a suitcase. Knowing there was a different agency watching my movements, I wanted them to know that someone had told me that I was being picked up.

However, no one showed up. After waiting a short period of time, I returned home. Then I checked my e-mail again. Now they sent me an e-mail that expressed their anger. They told me to "ditch the suitcase and bring only the File." One problem with that is I never had the File. Once again, I got on the phone with my mother. I was not able to discuss my case with anyone except my computer guy and my mother. Their reaction by the follow-up e-mail sent chills up my spine. Whoever was trying to lure me to pick me up was not interested in my safety, only that damn File! Technically, I needed to play one agency against the other in order to expose those who had wrong intentions. When someone is fleeing from their life, one needs to keep a clear head. Knowing everything that I did, I needed to keep questioning what was happening. Packing a suitcase that night set off a red flag to the agency that was monitoring my actions. Then when I had the discussion about the events over the phone, a different agency became aware of what was going on. All they had to do was to see where the two e-mails originated from. Then they would know who was behind the threats.

A few days later on Wednesday, December 7, 2005, at 8:38 PM, I received another message. This time, the message said,

"Hack:: Our sincere apologies to the Alamo we believe this matter is now under control." These words, although meant to be reassuring, did not bring me much comfort. My gut was telling me otherwise. I was told they had arrested dozens of people who were working on my case.

A short while later at 8:53 PM, I was sent the following explanation.

> *"(Hack:: Non-Official Cover Officers (NOCs), Official Cover Officers and Agent/Assets have played an important role in this ongoing case. This has been cause for much confusion on the part of both Active and Non-Active persons regarding this case. Such matters have been reorganized. Therefore any and all further confusion should be relinquished on both sides. Several operatives have been retained from opposing forces and should contain further damages. Again our most sincere apologies go out to the Alamo)"*

Once again it seemed as though I were drowning in chaos. Many times, the terrorists came so close to me. Being fearful of them was not an option to me. Standing up to them helped expose who they were. After all, we should "not fear those who kill the body but cannot destroy the soul," and we should not fear man. That does not mean that we are completely safe. We still need to be "cautious as serpents."

Then on Friday, December 16, 2005, I received the following message.

> *"Hack:: All acounted for RE: electronic mail. Please submit all further transmissions to my SEC407 accnt for analysis. Re: threat, It would be prudent for you to accept the protection offer we spoke about. This will prevent further harrassment toward the recipient. Arrangements are on hold."*

For some reason, they were unwilling to stop harassing me. The more that I remained silent, the more danger I was in. After all, I did not have any written agreements with anyone within the government. Therefore, I was under no legal obligations to them. Although the case was classified, I was not prohibited in any way of making my story public. Since they had not treated me by the law, never explained my rights to me or what I could and could not talk about, and did not have a signed contract with them, I have no accountability to them. After all, it seems as though many who were working on my case were not accountable either. Operation Firewall broke the news about the warrantless wiretaps. They have violated all of my rights. They used my name on the original warrant and then referred to the case number on all of the subsequent warrants. As a result, the government started to dictate and threaten many businesses including Microsoft, AOL, Yahoo! Coyote Cable Connections, Roadrunner, and Adelphia to name a few. It is one thing to put laws on the books and make these companies accountable for what happens through their Web sites, servers, and computers. It is a totally different thing when they threaten to put them out of business and then take some stock in their company in exchange for leniency.

As a side note, I found out that Microsoft had hired Daniel Polk on a previous occasion in order for him to track down who had sent out a big virus, I think it was the Love Bug virus. For two weeks' worth of work, he was paid handsomely. Then partway into the investigation, the government had discovered that Microsoft not only had vulnerabilities in their Windows system, but they were also secretly spying on the government. This came from a hacker who played one side against the other to his own monetary benefit.

Once the government learned of this, they switched all their computers over to Linux. What made Microsoft think that by hiring a professional hacker they would be honest in all their dealings? What made the government of the United States think the same thing? What if, being that Daniel Polk worked for Microsoft, he himself set them up to make it look like they were spying on the government? He could have been acting as a double agent, just like he did in my case, to his benefit. Then he could get paid from both ends and create himself more work, thus meaning job security.

When they had learned of his behavior and shipped him off for further interrogation, I thought that would be the end of him meddling in my affairs. After all, my computer guy had received notification that he and the three others had been executed. How do I believe anything that anyone was telling me? Too many times, they had lied to me. How was my computer guy supposed to believe everything he was being told as well?

At 10:52 PM, he received the following message.

> *"Hack: I have reason to believe that my earlier assumption is correct. Please reconsider my offer! The organization involved may not be totally conatined for a few weeks. Please do not worry about the alamo as that is under complete control. As a friend I am asking you to reconsider."*

My computer guy opted not to take the protection. He had suffered from several heart attacks already. Realizing that he had no control of his life, he decided to stay put.

All I know is that I wanted the whole thing to end. On December 23, 2005, they closed my case. However, all the other cases would still be ongoing for an indefinite period of time. It was music to my ears. The last figures that I had received were that over four thousand investigations resulted and over sixty-four thousand people arrested.

It seemed as though my computer guy only cared about himself. He did not take their advice to take the protection. He was warned that further harassment would continue to me as long as he was in the picture. Upon analyzing the previous e-mails, I noticed discrepancies in the way my computer guy was speaking. In one of the chats, where I had quoted text from the e-mail, it said, "Thus, for example, an individual who alleges that an employee has failed to adhere (Be advised, you may be called to testify in US Supreme Court in Washington DC on or about 16/01/06 notification to follow) to laws and regulations."

Then he said the following,

mrmagoo7: if one of the guys in the group . . . .

mrmagoo7: had me go into the server illegally . . . .

mrmagoo7: before a warrant was issued or some other technicality . . . . Ash's the oil off until I

mrmagoo7: i plead the fifth on everything

mrmagoo7: are they perceiving this as me accusing one of the guys

mrmagoo7: did something wrong, or protecting one of them

One could only conclude that he was being called to testify against one of the employees, probably Daniel Polk. However, the message later came that his privileges were suspended and his order of protection had been revoked. Now we began to interpret that they had changed their minds and decided to bring charges against him. How could they bring charges against him using the code of ethics for employees if he had not been an employee of the government? That would mean he has not been totally honest with me.

During this whole ordeal, there was no human being that I could completely trust. Somehow my street smarts, intuition, and my God were guiding me through the case. When they closed my case on December 23, 2005, after all that had happened, I still felt unsure of my life. My body felt like it was ready to collapse. A few weeks prior to this, I had suffered something that left me unable to move for quite a while at work. The stress of everything was taking its toll on my health.

A few days later after my case was closed, I received another threat. This was the straw that broke the camel's back. I decided that I needed to go public. Going public would put the light on the people responsible. It would be more of a protection to be out in the public. Remaining quiet only seemed to put me in more danger. In January of 2006, I sent out a press release by e-mail and fax to several news agencies and media. I also posted something on the Internet about the ordeal in order to redirect everyone's thinking.

Chapter 15

Going Public

$\mathcal{H}$ere is the Internet posting.

Cases as big as this one take time to get to the bottom of. Happily, I can report that my people have been very aggressive in this investigation. There are 1000's of people working on this case. Let me fill you all in on a few things.

In April of 2003, I had discovered that my computer had been hacked. When the police told me that it would take 3 months before they could look at my case, I decided to take matters into my own hands by starting my own investigation. The hackers started contacting me through instant messages trying to play head games with me by telling me that they were stalking me. I then went on a mission to learn how hackers work, the programs used, how they think, etc. to figure out by whom and how this was being done. I met this one computer programmer who changed my life. He had all the right connections.

The investigation ended up putting me into the witness protection program, the "watchful eye" version. I had never heard of this division before. Actually it ended up being another term for the "domestic spy program." The only reason it was "watchful eye" is because they thought I was having dealings with terrorists overseas? I never had phone service for international calls my whole life and do not know anyone living overseas and do not know any terrorist! In fact, the only people they were spying on were two, honest, American citizens. Our CIVIL rights as well as the rights of 1000's of American people have been VIOLATED right by our own American government. My people all have the proof of this!

In June of 2003, they code named the investigation "Operation Firewall," case number SSC_2003R01260.

Happily, I can report that over 64000 people were arrested as a result of the investigation. Over 4000 investigations spawned off the original one. Some cases are still ongoing. Many new laws, hundreds, have been put on the books for computer internet crimes and identity theft. However, some of the people who are supposed to enforce these new laws are the ones actually behind the identity theft themselves. We know who they are!

This took me 3 pain staking years of hours upon hours, night after night, on the computer to figure out who and what and how this was all being done. As a result, I have lost a ton of money in actual losses, time, and lost business and wages. Yet my people have saved the US government and insurance companies, and credit card companies over $265 billion a year of theft and not even a thank you!

I realize that writing this report online and posting it VOIDS any so-called "protection" I was "supposedly" under. In fact, I never saw any agreement or anything in writing from them. However, I have e-mails from the FBI (Federal Bureau of Investigation), CIA (Central Intelligence Agency, DOJ (Department of Justice), United States Security and Exchange Commission, SSC (Secret Service Commission) etc., In fact, I received correspondence directly from my "protectors" speaking to me through text taken from websites. When someone is in the witness program, they are not supposed to be in contact with the person. BIG MISTAKE! Also, I had a visit to my house by one of the "protectors" guised under "another identity." However, he used his real credit card number, address and phone number which gave me his real identity. A simple Google search resulted in more information. It was not until later in the year that I mentioned the name of this guy to my computer guy who told me that he was the head of the Department of Justice who was heading my case. This was the same guy who tried to set up my computer guy to testify! Come to find out, he was put up to this by someone else. The government then took him out of the DOJ and placed him in one of those "secret torture prisons." (If I were you, I would let him out now before we rescue him out of your prison.)

I would also like Google to know that the government already controls your search engine. Proof is on my computer! They used your search engine and stories to communicate information to me so that I could help them with their investigation. In fact, several TV shows, such as a TNT show called "The Closer" which is based after my case; all has been done without my consent. A reward was never offered. Instead, multiple DEATH ATTMEPTS have been made on my life. Going public is the only way to stay safe at this moment.

Anyway, in the middle of the investigation, they came across a file in one of the hackers computers. This file contained all of the security identification plates as well as money plates for the whole world! This included the plates used to make badges for the FBI, CIA, DOJ, USSEC, UN etc as well as the plates used for identification cards for Department of Motor Vehicles, Social Services, Social Security, etc. The code name for this investigation was "Abel Danger."

The file had been handed over to the US government. However, the key for the file was handed over to the United Nations who had purchased the file on the black market illegally. Without the key, the file was useless to the United States government. Therefore, George Bush made an agreement with the United Nations to purchase the key and not press any charges against the U.N. for the theft. The file was originally purchased by the U.N. for $140,000,000 on the black market. The United States wanted to make sure that the file was returned in its entirety. The U.N. was also really hurting for money, so they made a deal with the U.S. to sell them the key. (Follow the money trail) Everything comes down to greed when it comes to crime. What a motive for death attempts!

Upon opening the file, they discovered it was the "full version," but the text containing who owned the File was missing. That made them nervous that someone else knew about the illegal ownership of the File. Therefore, the U.S. went out and hired hit men to come after me. I had been given a partial copy of the File from my computer guy just in case something was to happen to him when he had to testify about the File. Then I could go PUBLIC to expose them. However, that did not happen either. (Don't you know who you are fighting?)

I am in the "witness protection plan" now but not the one from the U.S. government! No one can even get anywhere close to me to hurt me. The only reason they sealed "Operation Firewall" and classified my name was to shut me up so that I would not come forward with the story, which in turn would protect their "indiscretions."

The "Design-a-Site" scam resulted as an investigation from "Operation Firewall." Since the investigation is ongoing at this moment, I cannot go into the details, but I will make sure everyone knows as soon as possible.

Any reporters interested in seeking the full version of the story are welcome to contact me.

I would like to clarify a few things. The statement that I made, "If I were you, I would let him out now before we rescue him out of your prison," did not mean that I wanted all charges dropped. It meant that I did not want him to get off easy. They had told us that the four of them had been executed. For some strange reason, I still believed they were alive. Secondly, the partial file of the original File was what was on the CD that my computer guy gave me prior to him having to testify at the CIA building. I had no idea what was on that CD until after his testimony. He told me they were only partial copies of the plates and that it contained the text that proved the ownership of the File. If for some reason this partial copy had gotten into the wrong hands, no one would be able to use the copies of the plates since only half of the original plates were there. He only meant for this to be used in the event that he was incarcerated. In a sense this was his get-out-of-jail free card. Since he was the victim in this case, there should be no reason for them to press charges against him.

The following day upon returning home from work, my side door to the house was ajar, literally open several inches. My first thought was to see if the dog was all right. I noticed that the dog was not walking to greet me. Upon entering the bedroom, I noticed that my computer, the hard drive, was gone. All my papers and my desk were on the floor. I immediately called the local police department. Then I called my mother. While on the phone with her, I walked through the house just to make sure no one was still inside. Everything in the house was still here. Nothing else had been taken.

When the police arrived, I filled out a police report. Telling them very little, I documented that due to the fact that I was involved in a government investigation, there were programs that had been installed on my computer by them in order to track the hackers. I was told not to give these programs to anyone. It was clearly told to me that these programs could not get into the hands of the terrorists.

The following day, I went online to post what had happened and use reverse psychology to get my computer back. The posting said the following:

> National Security has been compromised. President Bush needs to step forward to show people that the Domestic Spy Program can be a positive tool!

> You will not believe what has happened to me in the past few days. I posted an update to my page here on Monday. In the text, I mentioned that I had evidence on my computer.

> When I arrived home from work on Tuesday, the following day, I had found out that my whole hard drive, the CPU, had been stolen. How convenient that it was stolen the day after my posting.

> I am happy to report that the police are investigating. I even tried calling the White House to let them know about the theft. However, it does not seem important enough for the president or one of his associates to return my call.

> However, he should be concerned. There was a program on my hard drive from the government, one that is only used and developed by the government

and cannot get into the hands of the terrorists. This program I used during the investigation. I was told not to pass it along to anyone outside the country, which no one has to worry about since I have no dealings with anyone outside the country.

I do believe that there are many good people in the government that did what was right to help me. However, some wrong people got involved along the way, including someone who read this posting on Monday.

Unknowingly, my neighbor had installed surveillance cameras several months earlier. The tape has been turned over to the police.

I am begging George Bush to step forward and do what is right. Even though my civil rights were violated by the U.S. government, at this time the NSA can do what is right and reverse the situation. Satellite pictures of my house can prove who is guilty and who is not involved.

Initially, when I believed that I was in the witness protection program, I did not have any problem with the government listening in on my phone lines, watching my home and working from satellites, and the body guards who were following me since I believed that all of this was being done in order to protect me. If you are doing what is right, there is no reason to feel like any of this would infringe on your rights.

Unfortunately, someone had leaked my name and information to the wrong people. I have had so many contradictory reports from the government's people.

I appreciated that the president told me yesterday in his speech that he is behind full disclosure of what is going on in the White House. He was very positive about the domestic spy program. Now he has the opportunity to step forward and put his actions behind his words. I believe that he will do this.

If they were in my shoes, they would realize that I am frustrated since I cannot seem to get justice. An apology would be sufficient.

By the way, the government can find my computer easily. The program on it reports to the government every time the computer goes online. I am begging George Bush to step forward and show the people that the NSA and domestic spy program can be used for something good.

I baited the "bad" people by saying this information was all on my computer. It worked. I had to do this to get the attention of George Bush. They took the bait and stole my hard drive. I hope they are not disappointed since any pertinent information was encrypted. Most of my hard drive had been backed up. There was nothing of any significance on the hard drive. Most of my documentation is spread out with many people. I am not stupid like they thought I would be. I told them exactly what I wanted them to believe just as I did the hackers, and they fell for it. Now they will get caught!

Happily, I can say they will be highly disappointed with their lack of findings. The coded e-mails, disguised as spam, cannot be interpreted by anyone else except the government and me. It will not mean anything to them without the backup documentation that is *not* on the computer. I would like for George Bush or his associate to contact me to work with me just as we had over the past three years. A lot of positive things have resulted from it.

The only thing I would have done differently if I were the government was to deal with me directly and not through anyone. They would have been surprised what I might have agreed to it. In fact, the terrorists never stopped my communication with the government. I needed them to think they did so they could leave me alone.

The program that is on my machine can be used to trace who and where they are. There is also the option of shutting the program down by destroying it from the government's end to maintain national security.

We need to maintain dialogue. The terrorists are crafty but are no challenge to my criminal-law education. Please contact me in writing or by phone, and I will be happy to continue our dialogue as we had previously. That way they have no clue as to what is going on at all since they cannot understand the coded language that we used.

By the way, check the phone calls I have received from so many so-called mortgage brokers of which some are the enemy. They were trying to pick my brain for knowledge and what I thought about the U.S. government. So I told them what I needed them to believe.

Please monitor my credit report as all my personal information was on my computer and the "wrong" people are watching it.

These people are counting on breaking my communication with the government.

I need for everyone to know that I never had any dealings knowingly with anyone who was a terrorist. However, a file worth $140,000,000, which the terrorists believed I had, attracted many of them around me in many different forms. They tried poison, incarceration, and killing me. Nothing has worked. In fact, their plan backfired.

The only way to beat the terrorists is first to learn how they think and work. Once you do that, they cannot control your mind and terrorize you. They lost! LOL, I do *not* mind being their bait (evidently they are attracted to the package)! LOL! They cannot get to me. Sometimes the best way to get into their minds is to make them think they got something they were after.

I will keep everyone updated.

At least now, the hackers might decide to leave me alone. If someone had my computer, then I had nothing left for them to take. Now maybe I would have some real peace.

*　　*　　*

About two weeks later, someone broke into my house and returned the computer. This time, they did not even try to access the bedroom where the dog was. To this day, I am not sure if they had physically injured the dog or had given her an injection. She was sore for several days. No obvious bruises were found. This would lead me to believe that she had been injected with a needle. That would be the only way to get past her. No one in their right mind would enter a house where there was a German shepherd unless they could subdue her. Just knowing that someone had entered my house again made me feel uneasy and sick to my stomach. If I ever find out who hurt my dog, I vow revenge!

*　　*　　*

In February of 2006, I went to the post office to pick up my job's mail. As I turned to leave from the post office counter, a man had entered the post office and came toward me. He was so angry and his face was beet red. Mentally and emotionally, fear came over me; but physically peace came over me, and I could not move or utter a word. I just stayed there and smiled. It was as if my smile was frozen on my face. Within five feet of me, he turned and veered off to his right. All of a sudden, I was able to move in order to exit the building.

All day, all that I could think about was what had happened at the post office. Although physically I could not respond during the incident, mentally and emotionally I was panicking. I could not understand why.

Several days later, it dawned on me why I felt that way. I phoned my computer guy and told him why. The guy was a spitting image of Daniel Polk! He told me that was impossible since he was one that had been executed. Knowing how they had lied to me on numerous occasions, I asked him to verify that it was not him.

After contacting Kermit, he reiterated that it could not be him. However, he said that my intuition was usually right. He agreed to check into it. A few days later, he contacted my computer guy, apologizing profusely. He swore that he was told that Daniel had been killed. However, once again I was right. They had just released him from prison a few weeks after his initial arrest. The government put a criminal back on the street. Instead of imprisoning him, they let him loose. That was him who came into the post office that day. That is something I will never forget.

Numerous months went by peacefully. About a year later, I received another threat. This time I decided to send the backup documentation with my story on CD. Once I sent that to the media, I have not heard another word. Finally, I had peace in my life.

Subconsciously at different times of the year, the past replays in my head. The reason for this book is to get my feelings and thoughts down on paper. This way, I can regain control of my life. By writing down these memories, it is a way of removing them from my head. Sometimes, watching the news riles up some of those memories, especially the stories related to identity theft.

Of the over four thousand investigations that were started during my case Operation Firewall, quite a few are still open. Some of the sixty-four-thousand-plus people are still awaiting sentencing.

When your back is against the wall and you are fighting for your life, sometimes the things you say and do at the moment do not make sense. However, in the end, things seem to work out. At least I came out of this experience with my life. Regaining my identity is taking much longer. Hopefully, one day shortly, my identity will be restored. Just because I do not share the same thoughts as the leaders of the United States that go to war and take lives do, it does not mean that I want any of those committing crimes not to pay for them. They do not deserve the easy way out through execution. They need to feel the anxiety and stress of fighting for their own lives. Death would be too easy of a way out.

Instead, the government lied and covered up the truth. It was hard to figure out what was the truth and what was not. The story of the man who was shot at the Miami Airport could not be verified. It was as if the whole incident was staged. There were no dates and times on the so-called Miami airport surveillance film. The story was sent to me two days before it supposedly happened. This story was used to try to deter us from exposing the truth. The threats that were sent to us were meant to scare us off. If we believed that he was really dead, then perhaps we would fear for our own lives even more.

Below is the text as it appeared in the e-mail from the Department of Justice.

Rigoberto Alpizar, a 44-year-old US citizen, was shot after fleeing an air marshal. No device has been found. Alpizar had arrived in Miami, Florida, from Ecuador and was boarding a flight to Orlando. (Hack:: Non-Official Cover Officers (NOCs), Official Cover Officers and Agent/Assets have played an important role in this ongoing case. This has been cause for much confusion on the part of both Active and Non-Active persons regarding this case. Such matters have been reorganized. Therefore any and all further confusion should be relinquished on both sides. Several operatives have been retained from opposing forces and should contain further damages. Again our most sincere apologies go out to the Alamo)

It is the first time since the attacks of 11 September 2001 that a US air marshal has shot at a passenger. The US dramatically increased the number of air marshals on flights after the 2001 attacks. Local police and federal officers are investigating the incident, but officials say so far there is no hint of any links to terrorism. However, as a precaution, federal air marshals were deployed in airports across the country.

'Appropriate action' Miami federal air marshal chief James Bauer told a press conference that the incident happened at about 1410 (1910 GMT). Aplizar, who was carrying a backpack and travelling with a woman thought to be his wife, had cleared customs and was boarding the Orlando flight, which originated in Medellin, Colombia. Shots were fired as the team attempted to subdue the subject Homeland security spokesman. At some point, he said "threatening words", Mr Bauer said. He was confronted by air marshals on board the flight, refused to comply with their demands and fled the aircraft. A spokesman for the homeland security department said he then reached into his bag, at which point, consistent with air marshal training, the air marshals "took the appropriate actions". "Shots were fired as the team attempted to subdue the subject," the spokesman said.

A witness told local television that the man frantically ran down the aisle of the Boeing 757 and that a woman with him said he was mentally ill and had not taken his medication. Television images showed police and emergency response officers surrounding the plane after the incident.

Later, investigators spread passengers' bags on the tarmac as sniffer dogs checked them for explosives. A man who claimed to have a bomb on board an American Airlines plane in Miami was shot dead by a US federal officer, officials say.

It was not until I found a picture of him on the Internet that my computer guy recognized who he was. However, he did not know him by the name of Rigoberto Alpizar. He was employed by the same cable company as my computer guy. He worked side by side with him on the jobs.

They also omitted facts from any of the news reports. The missing truckload of UPS tapes could have been stopped before the crime was even committed, or they could have picked up the truck once they saw that it was stolen. There has never been a follow-up news story about the outcome of the search of this truck.

The only reason they leaked Valerie Plame's name was to shut up her husband. They did not want him to go public with the information and proof that George Bush knew that he was going to war on false information. In other words, they would need to be put into the witness protection plan in order to hide the facts. There seems to be a common theme—hide the truth at any and all costs even if it means displacing or killing a human life.

Since they exposed my identity, I feel that it is justice to expose their plots. My case had originally been classified. Now it is my turn to tell my story, the truth. It has been told through my eyes as the way I had seen it. When you examine all the information, it is easier to make the right conclusions.

Chapter 16

The Results

buttercup71190: ur friends seem to have some pull

mrmagoo7: my friends could pull the carpet right out from under the government if they so chose

buttercup71190: wow

mrmagoo7: who do you think actually runs things

mrmagoo7: the government is run by computers . . . .

mrmagoo7: my friends run those computers!

buttercup71190: i know

buttercup71190: scary that u know so much lol

mrmagoo7: piss them off and we are all in the stone age

buttercup71190: lmao

mrmagoo7: well why do you think i get so nervous sometimes, its because i do know what i do

mrmagoo7: i'm very good at what i do because i am even more cautious about how i do it

buttercup71190: k

mrmagoo7: and besides i wouldnt take on a case for just anybody

buttercup71190: so y me then?

mrmagoo7: 5 words

mrmagoo7: because you are worth it!

mrmagoo7: i trusted you immediately

mrmagoo7: dont know why, just did

mrmagoo7: something about you told me deep down inside that i could trust you

mrmagoo7: so i listened

buttercup71190: was it the desperation in my voice?

mrmagoo7: no not at all

buttercup71190: was it because i knew brat? lol

mrmagoo7: yeah ok, going offline now, lol

buttercup71190: sa

mrmagoo7: but seriously . . . .

buttercup71190: so y?

mrmagoo7: ok, let me try to explain . . . .

mrmagoo7: what you may call "instinct" about someone that you meet, i call interpretation of emotional vibrations

buttercup71190: oh ok

mrmagoo7: i can feel things about people, always have

mrmagoo7: havent always been right, but damned close

buttercup71190: well i am thankful for all that you have done

buttercup71190: and ur friends

mrmagoo7: its like being tuned in to someone so much that you can sometimes finish

	their sentences, or feel their pain or their joy
mrmagoo7:	i think it is a sense we all have but most never tap into it or make use of it
mrmagoo7:	we are all connected, just a matter of finding the right frequency
mrmagoo7:	ok, enough of that, dont want you to think i'm a nut job
buttercup71190:	lol
mrmagoo7:	i dont share that philosophy with many people, only a few
mrmagoo7:	only the people i trust
mrmagoo7:	and that doesnt happen for me very often
buttercup71190:	u have brought some peace and sanity back into my life
buttercup71190:	the justice is going to be the cherry on top with whipped cream
mrmagoo7:	well you have helped me to justify my insanity, so i guess we are even
buttercup71190:	lol
buttercup71190:	is there ever going to be an end to all of this? or at least some closure of some sort?
mrmagoo7:	yes its already ended . . . . it just has to be finalized in court
buttercup71190:	the local part is not
mrmagoo7:	those people can no longer hurt you or anyone else any more
mrmagoo7:	well he is a big joke, he will be easier to deal with
mrmagoo7:	at least he is right out in the open
buttercup71190:	i am talking about my ex, coyote cable, gary, and my neighbor

mrmagoo7: we get your ex last darlin, i promise

buttercup71190: what do u think his role was in the whole thing?

mrmagoo7: and gary is just a schmuck, he is nothing but a simple con artist who got caught in the mix

mrmagoo7: dont know for sure, but if you really trust me, then you know i will find out

mrmagoo7: i'm not all about myself, but i do love a mystery

buttercup71190: coyote online was now bought out by someone

mrmagoo7: yes they are being forced to, its part of a deal they are making

buttercup71190: deal?

mrmagoo7: yes to get off easy

buttercup71190: y?

mrmagoo7: because they were not doing their jobs security wise

buttercup71190: so they are going to get off

buttercup71190: great

buttercup71190: that's only a slap

mrmagoo7: no they are losing their company, thats not getting off

buttercup71190: losing it?

mrmagoo7: yeah they aint making much on it

mrmagoo7: just enough to survive

mrmagoo7: and pay their bills

buttercup71190: and the people directly involved?

mrmagoo7: they are losing their jobs

buttercup71190: did u find out who yet?

mrmagoo7:   a few will stay with the new company until it uses them to learn their way around and train their own people

buttercup71190:   i am angry they are getting off

buttercup71190:   its not fair after all they did

intemrmagoo7:   you are not looking at the big picture . . . .

buttercup71190:   one of those ppl are a direct tie to my ex

mrmagoo7:   you will have won

mrmagoo7:   well in the end we may be able to prove that

buttercup71190:   i dont care about winning i want justice

buttercup71190:   they created so much trouble for me

mrmagoo7:   i think it is justice that a whole company as big as that will be swept away from them because they couldnt control it or their employees

buttercup71190:   its a start but they are getting off easy

mrmagoo7:   a lifetime of accumulated work is being taken away from them . . . . there is nothing easy about it

buttercup71190:   i hope they are changing some of those laws to make them more responsible; personally responsible would be a start

mrmagoo7:   some of those new laws are helping to take that company away from them

mrmagoo7:   its called leverage

buttercup71190: i would like to know who was all involved mrmagoo7:	well they will be out of work soon

mrmagoo7:	check the unemployment line, lol

mrmagoo7:	alot of people sacrificed a lot of time and money to accomplish this, you should be happy that this is being done

buttercup71190:	i am. i could have never done any of this on my own

buttercup71190:	i know one of them is linked to my ex and i want him personally pay for it

mrmagoo7:	just think if you tried to take on your cable company on your own, you would die of old age before anything would come of it

buttercup71190:	lol

mrmagoo7:	but because you made some real friends and reached the right people, your cable company will be no more

mrmagoo7:	so pat yourself on the back and be thankful that at least this happened

mrmagoo7:	sometimes in order to get the queen bee, you must destroy the whole hive my dear

buttercup71190:	ohhhhhhhhhhhh

buttercup71190:	who is the queen?

mrmagoo7:	just like the alamo

buttercup71190:	lol

mrmagoo7:	the queen is the guy at your cable company that pissed me off

buttercup71190:	who?

mrmagoo7:	and lied to me on the phone

mrmagoo7:	and never emailed me back

buttercup71190:	stuart

mrmagoo7:   yepper

mrmagoo7:   so now he's done

buttercup71190:   how was he involved?

mrmagoo7:   dont know, but he pissed me off, so i eliminated his job

buttercup71190:   what did he do?

mrmagoo7:   along with many others

mrmagoo7:   but i'm sure all the hard workers at the company will be absorbed into the new one

mrmagoo7:   he friggin lied to me by tellin me he was gonna do something, i dont like people blowing smoke up my ass

buttercup71190:   what was he supposed to do?

mrmagoo7:   he was supposed to resolve your problem and find out who was responsible at your cable company . . . . and he lied to me and never did it

mrmagoo7:   why do you think i was the one to go into their mail server

buttercup71190:   k

buttercup71190:   and u were able to see he was involved?

mrmagoo7:   yes, and it took me all of 8 mos to get my friends to back me on this and get the frigging warrent

mrmagoo7:   all i wanted was for stuart to find out the truth, he lied to me and it became personal

buttercup71190:   remind me never to piss u off lol

mrmagoo7:   remember a few months ago when i told you your cable company would be bought out?

buttercup71190:   that's how i feel about the person there that i think is tied to my ex

mrmagoo7:	you didnt believe me
buttercup71190:	its personal
buttercup71190:	i did
buttercup71190:	just didn't know how soon
mrmagoo7:	yes i realize that, but it is easier to take out alot of people all at once than to go after individuals . . . . thats what your case has been about from the minute my friends got involved
mrmagoo7:	they cant go after all these little guys with no proof, but put all these idiots together with their buddies and you have a court case worth winning
mrmagoo7:	and besides my dear you told me you wanted something tangible that you could see . . . .
mrmagoo7:	so i gave you Coyote Cable Connections
buttercup71190:	ty
mrmagoo7:	but left to their own devices without their jobs and separating all of them, they will make mistakes
buttercup71190:	i didnt get that last message
mrmagoo7:	i couldnt get any evidence on any particular people at coyote cable, but the company as a whole was responsible for some very serious security issues
buttercup71190:	what does that mean?
mrmagoo7:	serious enough to take down the company itself
buttercup71190:	they were hacking? eavesdropping? or what?
mrmagoo7:	lets just say that alot of viruses, trojans and hacking was being conducted by

too many people using your cable company as an isp

buttercup71190: k

mrmagoo7: not by your cable company's employees themselves, at least not that we can prove

buttercup71190: and Coyote Cable Connections did nothing about it except ignore it

mrmagoo7: they didnt just ignor it

mrmagoo7: they were helping, but we cant prove that, so they cant be prosecuted, but they can be forced to sell the company in order to avoid any further investigation

buttercup71190: oh

mrmagoo7: see and you thought you had no friends, lol

buttercup71190: i never said that

mrmagoo7: it was a joke darlin

buttercup71190: i am glad i do and the right ones at that

buttercup71190: i know

mrmagoo7: if ya cant take the fish outta the pond, then drain the pond

buttercup71190: lol

mrmagoo7: it may not be what you wanted, but it's a lot more effective

buttercup71190: i am not worried about what happens, i just want to see them squirm

buttercup71190: they being audited?

mrmagoo7: dont know

mrmagoo7: doubt it

buttercup71190: k

mrmagoo7:	course the companys books will be gone over with a fine tooth comb now
buttercup71190:	i can prove that they were aiding in hacking
mrmagoo7:	you already did
buttercup71190:	their friend hijacked my account lol
buttercup71190:	and the cops account
mrmagoo7:	your log files helped to make this happen
buttercup71190:	all the sbo's that came from them?
buttercup71190:	and remote activates
mrmagoo7:	not from them from people online with them, thats all we can prove
buttercup71190:	k
mrmagoo7:	if we had had mac addresses and stuff in your log files we could have tied everyone responsible
mrmagoo7:	but we didnt
buttercup71190:	y not?
mrmagoo7:	because your programs could not detect them thru coyote cable
buttercup71190:	oh
mrmagoo7:	your cable company had all the mac addresses, but we couldnt tie them together with the times and the IP's because they werent keeping their log files as required by law
mrmagoo7:	thats how we got em
buttercup71190:	they probably tried to delete incriminating evidence
buttercup71190:	so they are getting off easy now
mrmagoo7:	well just dont be too upset that you couldnt fry a couple of fish when we

drained the whole pond for you . . . .
its the best we could do

buttercup71190: i am not

buttercup71190: nothing in this case went as i thought
lol

mrmagoo7: be happy it was taken seriously and
something was done about it

buttercup71190: i am

mrmagoo7: and besides they are all out of business
and cant hurt anyone now

buttercup71190: but if he suspects that i was behind
Coyote Cable Connections' warrant,
he will

buttercup71190: and he does

mrmagoo7: well they dont suspect you

mrmagoo7: they suspected alot of possible people
including you, but that all vannished
when they found out how big this
was

buttercup71190: good lol

mrmagoo7: now they are just scrambling around
and hoping for jobs with the new
company and stepping all over each
other in the process

buttercup71190: lol

mrmagoo7: so many roaches and so few jobs,
lol

buttercup71190: i thought they are letting some go?

mrmagoo7: yes but none of them know who
yet

buttercup71190: oh

buttercup71190: so they have no clue

mrmagoo7: nope

buttercup71190: that they were caught

mrmagoo7:   but guess what, my old friend Stuart
                   Reynolds aint got even a chance of
                   getting a job, they dont need him

buttercup71190: cool

buttercup71190: any fines for not having the logs?

mrmagoo7:   i am hoping that your cable company
                   knowing who really is responsible for
                   what was done within the company
                   will take it out on them before the
                   sale

buttercup71190: oh

mrmagoo7:   selling the company will be enough
                   for the investigators

mrmagoo7:   no fines will be imposed

buttercup71190: k

mrmagoo7:   so i dont know about you . . . . you
                   have caused more trouble for more
                   people than any woman i know, hee
                   hee

buttercup71190: no, i could not have done it without
                   you or your friends. so you guys did.
                   lol

buttercup71190: all i did was figure it out

mrmagoo7:   you really should try to do things on
                   a smaller scale, lol

buttercup71190: u think?

Chapter 17

Justice Wanted

$\mathcal{L}$et me start by introducing myself. My name is Angela Hart, who resides in the beautiful Catskill Mountains in upstate New York. I am a single, disabled, female citizen of the United States who has had to endure many crimes against humanity from our own leaders of the United States of America. I am looking for closure. I would like justice, even if it means the conviction of the former president (George Bush) and the former vice president (Dick Cheney). I am also seeking a formal apology and some sort of restitution for my losses and time.

Here is the story of how I helped fight the war on terror without picking up a weapon.

In April of 2003, I discovered that my computer had been hacked and I had people stalking me. Several weeks later, I discovered that my identity had been stolen as well. Since the NYS Internet crime division could not get to my case for several months, I started my own investigation to gather evidence and leave a trail just in case the stalkers carried out their threats.

At that time, my new computer guy started working with a few of his friends, two of which worked for the Department of Justice and the other in the CIA. Operation Firewall began in July 2003 as an investigation in access device fraud before expanding into an investigation of global credit card fraud and identity theft fraud.

My computer guy did not tell me much about what was going on until the first forty-eight people were arrested on October 28, 2004.

Once that occurred, he filled me in about the investigation. I had worked well over a year with him retrieving all the evidence from my old computer; tracing all the IPs trying to access my computer; turning over log files; gathering pictures, names, phone numbers, and other pertinent information.

However, once people were arrested, I was told that I was placed in the witness protection program, the "watchful eye" version. My name had been used on the original warrant for Operation Firewall, but after that, only my case number was used on the other warrants. I had people supposedly assigned to me to stay within a certain distance. My phones were tapped. I was also told that I was under satellite surveillance.

I kept questioning if any of this was real since I never had spoken to any of those working on my case directly. Then in January of 2004, I had one of the investigators stay at my house since I rent the rooms out for income. I did not learn of his true identity for several months when I figured out who he was.

Some bizarre things started to happen around me. When I began to question it, I was then told about the File. The discovery of the File opened a new investigation that was code-named Abel Danger. I knew at this point, the contents of the file were attracting the wrong people. Over and over I expressed my concerns to my computer guy by e-mail, instant messaging, and phone, all of which were being monitored. I started documenting the events and continued to cry out for help. I did not realize the monetary value of this file until I was told what it contained. It contained actual copies of the plates used to make identification badges for the FBI, CIA, DOJ, USSEC, SSC, police, pass cards, etc.; plates used to make U.S. currency; plates to make false Medicare cards; Medicaid cards; a full set of plates to make false drivers licenses, passports, and any other identification cards you can think of! In fact, a computer that was found during the investigation led to the identification of the terrorists who attacked the twin towers on September 11, 2001. The story was on *20/20* or *Primetime*. This computer also led to a lot of other information that was never made public. It included a list of people who had prior knowledge of the attacks, which included government employees. During the investigation, when the File was found, they changed the U.S. currency again. They added many new features to printing money including the color.

By November of 2005, I had to stop all communication with my computer guy. We had worked on this case every day since Easter of 2003 to track and document everything, sometimes until two, three, or five in the morning! The reason I had to stop talking to him was because some people were sending me information that was making me believe that I could not trust him. Government officials started sending me information by e-mail disguised as spam, but with the seals embedded from the FBI, CIA, DOJ, USSEC, etc. Then I started receiving disturbing e-mails. Then I had people trying to book rooms then canceling. The tone of the voices and what they said made me feel like someone was putting them up to it. Perhaps the wrong people were trying to book and were not allowed by my protectors.

My computer guy had a signed contract with the government when he turned over the File to protect him and let him remain anonymous. The File had been found on one of the hacker's computers under a search warrant. Then several months later, he received a new contract, which he was not allowed to read or open until after he gave a deposition. The government had changed their mind. They did not send him the key to decrypt it until after the deposition. Then a few weeks later, this same guy sent him another e-mail saying that they were going to need his testimony. This time, the message sounded threatening, like they were going to bring him up on charges. We both helped the government work on this case for three years without ever getting paid. All evidence was turned over as we came across it. The File had been turned over. Everything we did was according to the law. Now we were being set up. Then the threats began to pour in.

One was against my computer guy. The government had made a deal with him to remain anonymous since the file contained very sensitive information and was worth $140,000,000 on the black market and was owned by the United Nations.

The first threat came in the link entitled *"dojj" xxxxxAny attempt to leave the United States will result in imediate apprehension"*. He was being called to testify about the File (Abel Danger); I had military helicopters circling outside my house to let him know that they wanted him to testify and make sure he did not leave the country. Using scare tactics on people, citizens who were trying to do the right thing, is not my idea of freedom.

At this point in time, my computer guy handed me an encrypted copy of a CD. I was told that if something happened to him, I was to give this to certain people. A friend of his had the key. So he went and testified at the CIA building about the file. Just as I had suspected, he had to plead the fifth when being asked about where the file was found, during Operation Firewall, which was classified at the time. At one point in time, they threw the cuffs on him to try to threaten him. He told the truth, only what he could testify to since Operation Firewall was classified and he was under the government's rules and regulations, and was released.

Now I knew that someone was trying to set him up. If you could not testify about where the File was found, wouldn't it look like you were trying to protect a terrorist? The plan almost worked.

Then the next threat came in the link titled *"dojji" (The illegal possession of government property can and will cost more than the price of ones freedom)*. The only way that I can interpret this is that the "cost" would be one's life. Now that is a threat! At this point in time, I asked my computer guy if he had a copy of the original CD. He told me he did. I talked him into turning it over. The next link, titled *"doji" said, "(Hack:: Request for Security Clearence is denied. Suspension of privilages will continue until further notice. Room unavailable at this time. Protection order has been revolked. Please remain inside the U.S. until Order is lifted)."*

Now my computer guy was being brought up on charges as a terrorist and was scheduled for his court date on 1/16/06.

Through a series of events, I figured out who was setting us up. In the summer of 2005, they gave me a security clearance with my name being "the Alamo." When they did this, I had remembered someone staying at my house during the previous winter that talked to me about the Alamo. This conversation stood out in my mind since I do not know many people who ever talk about the Alamo. I then went through my reservation book. Finding the name, Mike F. McCusker, I decided to verify the name and address and phone on the Internet. The general's name of the Alamo was Custer, which was close to the name used, Mike F. McCusker. The address and phone matched but the name did not. Daniel Polk was the right name. I then did a search on the name. After coming across a Web site that discussed his education, my gut was telling me that he was working on my case. This was the same person who had almost placed me in the witness protection plan by relocating me in August of 2005 because he thought someone had figured out his identity, not that I was in any danger at that point that I knew of. When my computer guy had received the deposition e-mail, I asked him if he knew who this person was. He told me that Daniel Polk was the head of the Department of Justice and he was heading my case. Then he proceeded to tell me that this is the same person who told him he had to be deposed. He knew that if my computer guy had to testify about the File, he could; but if anything came up about how the file was found, which was during Operation Firewall, he would have to plead the fifth since the investigation was supposedly classified. Then when my computer guy received the new e-mail that they wanted him to testify, I knew he was being set up! During testimony, he would not be allowed to plead the fifth unless he was willing to be locked up! After a long conversation with him on the phone that night, we received a letter of apology from the Department of Justice explaining that they were sorry for what was happening. Evidently, not only did he try to set us up to take the fall, but he had also tried to change the date on the File in order for the president to be able to use that as an excuse of why he went to war. However, they arrested Daniel Polk the day after he posted a false date for the File on the Internet. He was then sent to an undisclosed foreign prison camp sometime in November of 2005. Please see link titled *"cia"* *"We have Him."*

Then I received additional information contained in the link titled *"2doj"* (HACK:: *Please accept our sincere apology to you and Alamo for the events which unfolded in the previous weeks. The one responsible has been removed and transferred to an unknown location for further interrogation and will be prosecuted. Our thanks, <Kermit>*)

Internet addresses were forwarded to us where Daniel Polk had just posted information, the day before his arrest, trying to backdate the "File."

However, it was not until December that I had been given information that it was not only the president behind the plan. There was someone else still out there. There was also a ploy to get the president impeached. This "File," which was worth $140,000,000 to the United Nations since that is what they paid for it, made some people really greedy. After the greed, power became the driving force behind these scandals being exposed.

By now, things were getting really strange. I had been receiving the news feeds prior to them becoming public through these spam e-mails that were all in military lingo. Unless someone knew all the information about my case, these e-mails would look worthless. Then I had received one e-mail in particular to watch extra careful that Friday afternoon. At one point during the day, I had to go to the bank for work. While driving to the bank, which is only two miles away, the e-mails were being acted out. I can describe what happened verbally much better than I can write this. People who were supposedly protecting me, watching is the better word to describe it, were exposing who they were to me. One guy on the side of the road caught my eye in particular. It was the same guy who had come to my house on four other occasions posing as a life insurance salesman. He was on the side of the road, talking to someone with no briefcase or anything in his hands like he was a salesman. In fact, I had company at my house on a few of the occasions that he had shown up. I did not like the feeling or vibe I got from him. In fact, I filed a complaint with the life insurance company so that he cannot go to my house again.

Then on that Sunday, my mom and I went out for breakfast at the local diner. While there numerous people had come in, some of whom I recognized as my "protectors." However, the guy in the back was the same person that was talking to the insurance salesman on the side of the road. After listening to several conversations that contained text from the e-mails, I knew something was up. Later that day, I had a conversation with my mom on the phone to discuss what had happened. Since the phones were being monitored, I wanted the higher-ups to know everything. A few days later, I received an e-mail once again from the Department of Justice acknowledging that once again they were sorry for what had happened. They said they had straightened that matter out. It resulted in the arrest of dozens of people working on my case to protect me. The first link sent to me in this response was *12/7/05 (Hack:: Our sincere apologies to the Alamo we believe this matter is now under control.)*.

Further explanation was given in the next e-mail link *"12-7-05B" (Hack:: Non-Official Cover Officers (NOCs), Official Cover Officers and Agent/Assets have played an important role in this ongoing case. This has been cause for much confusion on the part of both Active and Non-Active persons regarding this case. Such matters have been reorganized. Therefore any and all further confusion should be relinquished on both sides. Several operatives have been retained from opposing forces and should contain further damages. Again our most sincere apologies go out to the Alamo).*

Then I started receiving e-mails from people that were making me believe that I needed to be picked up and placed into the witness protection plan since I had all this danger around me. However, the tone started to change when they told me to bring only the CD (File) and nothing else. Evidently, some people thought I had a copy of the "File," which I did not. I then realized that I was in much more danger than I had realized. The carbon monoxide problems at my house became possible death attempts in their eyes. The poisoning of the milk in my refrigerator might also have been. I also had a few other incidents, which I could never positively prove, happen.

Next I received another e-mail containing the following: *"kerm1" (Hack:: All acounted for RE: electronic mail. Please submit all further transmissions to my SEC407 accnt for analysis. Re: threat, It would be prudent for you to accept the protection offer we spoke about. This will prevent further harrassment toward the recipient. Arrangments are on hold)*

Kerm2 said (Hack: I have reason to believe that my earlier assumption is correct. Please reconsider my offer! The organization involved may not be totally conatined for a few weeks. Please do not worry about the alamo as that is under complete control. As a friend I am asking you to reconsider)

The final text received *"lastalamo" Hack:: Security clearance deniedaccepted meet point to follow good bye.* He then turned over the CD. I then asked him what was on the CD that he gave me. James told me that it was a partial stripped copy that contained the owner information of the "File." He felt that having this partial copy was his ticket to make sure that nothing happened to him when he went to testify at the CIA building.

Then in January, I decided to go public with the story. Since I could not get anyone to get me out of the situation or protect myself, going public is the only way that I can stay safe. Being quiet was putting me in too much danger.

Somewhere along the line, my name was leaked, either by the Department of Justice or the CIA. I am under no legal contracts or obligations to anyone at this point.

I do believe that many good people were helping me along the way. However, at some point in time, the wrong people got involved. By the way, someone else had told me that the "watchful eye program" was nothing more than a glorified name for the "domestic spy program."

Since nothing was ever in writing or signed by me, both the government and myself are not protected. My rights have been violated. I have suffered many losses along the way. It has affected my life forever. Both my businesses were shut down off the net, hacked, and no one offered to replace them for me. I do not have the money to reinvest into the sites. In fact, I am still paying off the loans that I used to start the business for the next five years.

I had sent out a press release to the major news stations and newspapers, stating only basic information but connecting the dots for them. I mentioned that I had some of the information on my computer. The day after the press release went out and post went onto the Internet, my home was broken into, and the computer hard drive was stolen. My identity has been stolen again, and I lost some personal stuff. However, anything on my computer that was important was backed up and in other locations with other people. Some of the information was encrypted. No one else would be able to understand the information without knowing other facts and events. The only things of any value on the computer were the government programs that were being used to trace everything. I was told that I could not give any of the programs to anyone. There was one in particular that I was told that could not get into terrorists' hands. Therefore, it became a matter of national security since someone had stolen these programs.

The following day after I posted some information on the Internet, I then did a follow-up post. Using reverse psychology, I was able to get my computer back within two weeks. Story after story began to unfold in the national news. The government began to fight among themselves and start to crumble. More and more information began to leak.

Recently, George Bush made the comment that he does not like it when "classified" information is leaked. However, there is a double standard. It is okay to leak the information when he himself does it!

I would like to set the record straight and prevent the president from changing history! The File was found in July of 2003, several months after the war started. Daniel Polk was asked to back date the File so that the president could use it as the reason why he went to war. I would hate to think that the File would be used for that reason! Since it was found during my original case, Operation Firewall, I would feel really guilty if he did use it as a reason to go and have people killed! The File was saved with the original case number for Operation Firewall. In fact, once Daniel Polk was first arrested in November of 2005, the CIA sent an e-mail and sent us the link of the Web site he had first listed, the File being used with a different date. He is the person who was fired, not the name of the other woman you first thought.

As a side note, in January of 2006, my computer guy received a call from one of his friends and was told that Daniel Polk and three others had been sent to those prison camps and executed. However, in February of 2006, I ran into someone in the post office who came at me with extreme anger. I just looked in his eyes and he walked right past me. It did not hit me until three days later that the guy was a spitting image of Daniel Polk. When I mentioned this to my computer guy, he said that was impossible since he was dead. However, he mentioned it to his friend. He then looked into the matter. Several days later, we were told that he was alive and well and had been released from the prison.

Remember, Valerie Plame's name was leaked only when her husband was going to go public with information prior to going to war to let people know that the president was basing his decision on faulty information and that the president knew it was. Therefore, the president ordered her name leaked. Then the only option would be to send them *both* into the witness protection plan.

After witnessing what the government did to me by exposing my name and identity, I decided to go public. The "witness protection plan" only protects the government's secrets and not the people they are supposed to protect. Since they did nothing by the law or the book, it actually gives me the freedom of speech by putting me under *no obligation* to them about anything. They have no legal recourse against me. I guess that's why they tried to have me killed instead. Their efforts have failed repeatedly. I wonder if someone higher up is watching over me.

I did nothing but try to help this government. I gave them a lot of my time tracking these hackers, my old computer, all my log files, and many other things. I allowed them to install programs on my computer to do all of this.

As a side note, I have never been arrested for any misdemeanor or felony, never been to jail, and never committed any other crime. I have never owned any firearms. However, over the past six years, I have been living in my own hellhole/concentration camp in the sense that I have had to endure many trials and circumstances. I am now going to put an end to it. I am tired of their threats. *I want justice!!!*

I am enclosing copies of their threats and correspondences to substantiate my claims. Please feel free to use my information in any way that you see fit to make public this information. Threats of sanctions, death wishes, and acts of terrorism will not stop me!

The text in the seals can be copied and pasted into Microsoft Word. Then select all, pick black print to read. Perhaps you may want to use the phrases and wordings in the seal and do a Google search. The partial File sent contains code to let the government and United Nations know when it is being viewed. Please save all Word documents to a portable drive; then the other File will not be on the net. The key to the File lies within a book cover. I did not say that it would all be that easy, but it will be well worth the effort. The *Alamo* refers to me and *Hack::* or *Mrmagoo7* refers to my computer guy and *ex* refers to Daniel Polk.

Operation Firewall resulted in the arrest of over sixty-four thousand people. These include over four thousand investigations. It shut down three major Web sites involved in the sale of people's identities. The T-Mobile incident with Paris Hilton's address book was the same hacker that was in my machine. I should say one of the original seven hackers. The huge identity thefts, with MasterCard/Visa, were also one of the cases that resulted. The Bank of America identity thefts came about the same way. There were many other stories that came out during that time that were all tied to this case. One was the tapes from Equifax that were being transported by truck; which ended up missing. The one thing that really upsets me about this government was the news story that was published about that missing truck. What they did not tell you was that they knew about the theft before it happened since they were under investigation already. They know exactly where it all is. Has anyone ever heard if the truck was found or if the information was turned back over to the rightful owners, or did someone get paid off to shut up or knocked off?

Remember the story about the man that was killed at the Miami airport? The CIA sent us the story in an e-mail within their seal the day before the guy was supposedly killed. It is in the Links folder under 12_7_05B.html. See the message to Hack:: within the seal to see who this guy was. Somehow, the guy killed, Rigoberto Alpizar, was involved in this case since he worked alongside my computer guy at the same cable company. The whole story never came out. The real story that needs to come out is that the former president and vice president are two of the biggest terrorists in the world and they are running our country! All the news is scrutinized and rewritten several times before the information goes public. The United Nations is involved up to their necks and is going to go down with this government as well. They are not the peace-seeking organization they claim to be unless death is part their way of attaining peace. That is the only way they know how to make someone shut up to protect themselves. Some of the news feeds that I was allowed to read before they went public would send chills up your spine!

Now you have the chance to right some of the many wrongs by publishing the real story and doing your own investigation. You thought Watergate was big? All I know is that I am tired of all the lies and deception and want the truth to come out. Over four thousand investigations started as a result of the initial one, Operation Firewall. Over sixty-four thousand were arrested. Web sites such as Cruising-the-Shadows and CardingCrew were shut down. The last figure I received was that the arrest of everyone resulted in the savings and confiscation of property that resulted in over $260 billion ($260,000,000,000) per year. I would like to know where all the money is going since there were many victims in this case who had their identities stolen and received many other grievances in their lives, and no one has been compensated for their troubles. Also, with that amount of money being found, why are not the insurance companies getting repaid for all their losses and then passing the savings on to the consumer who first paid for it all in the beginning? Many people suffered as a result of these terrorists and should be repaid.

I am asking that further prosecution of George Bush and Dick Cheney be sought for war crimes and crimes against humanity. In fact, I also have a copy of the code of ethics for the government. Since they broke these laws repeatedly, they should be prosecuted to the fullest extent of the law.

It is very ironic that our current president is now considering handing over the sovereignty of the United States to the United Nations. This seems to be in admission that he does not know how to lead the country. Instead, he is handing the power over to the United Nations.

We, the people, should exercise our rights and take back our country, for that matter, take back the world.

Sincerely,

Angela Hart

Index

Edwards Brothers,Inc!
Thorofare, NJ 08086
20 December, 2010
BA2010354